SCIENCE FOUNDATIONS

Matter and Energy

SCIENCE FOUNDATIONS

The Big Bang
Cell Theory
Electricity and Magnetism
Evolution
The Expanding Universe
The Genetic Code
Germ Theory
Gravity
Heredity
Kingdoms of Life
Light and Sound
Matter and Energy
Natural Selection
Planetary Motion
Plate Tectonics
Quantum Theory
Radioactivity
Vaccines

SCIENCE FOUNDATIONS

Matter and Energy

P. ANDREW KARAM AND BEN P. STEIN

CHELSEA HOUSE
An Infobase Learning Company

Science Foundations: Matter and Energy

Copyright © 2011 by Infobase Learning

Chelsea House
An imprint of Infobase Learning
132 West 31st Street
New York, NY 10001

Library of Congress Cataloging-in-Publication Data
Karam, P. Andrew.
  Matter and energy / by P. Andrew Karam and Ben P. Stein.
      p. cm. — (Science foundations)
  Includes bibliographical references and index.
  ISBN 978-1-60413-345-5 (hardcover)
  1. Matter—Popular works. 2. Force and energy—Popular works. I. Stein, Ben P. II. Title. III. Series.
  QC171.2.K37 2011
  530—dc22   2010026880

You can find Chelsea House on the World Wide Web at
http://www.chelseahouse.com

Text design by Kerry Casey
Cover design by Alicia Post
Composition by EJB Publishing Services
Cover printed by Yurchak Printing, Inc., Landisville, Pa.
Book printed and bound by Yurchak Printing, Inc., Landisville, Pa.
Date printed: April 2011
Printed in the United States of America

10 9 8 7 6 5 4 3 2 1

This book is printed on acid-free paper.

All links and Web addresses were checked and verified to be correct at the time of publication. Because of the dynamic nature of the Web, some addresses and links may have changed since publication and may no longer be valid.

Contents

1   Introduction to Matter and Energy   7

2   What Matter Is   11

3   What Energy Is   24

4   Classical Ideas of Energy   38

5   Einstein's Revolution: Matter Is "Frozen" Energy   48

6   Particle Explosion   59

7   Matter and Energy in the Universe   74

8   New Matter and Energy   87

9   Why Is There New Matter?   100

Glossary   112

Bibliography   115

Further Resources   116

Picture Credits   118

Index   119

About the Authors   124

Introduction to Matter and Energy

The universe contains just two things: matter and energy. **Matter** makes up almost everything imaginable—furniture, food, houses, rocks, living organisms, and the whole Earth. **Energy** is not as easy to see—hands cannot hold pure energy—but it powers racecars, makes living things move, and travels distances ranging from the confines of an **atom** to the ends of the universe. Light is an example of pure energy. A falling rock gains energy as it falls. People purchase energy in the form of electricity to **power** their homes. On the surface, it seems simple—matter can be grasped and energy can't.

In reality, things are much more complex. Albert Einstein showed that matter can become energy, and energy can turn into matter. They can change into one another under certain circumstances. This fact, discovered just over a hundred years ago, changed the world not only for scientists, but for everyone: For example, less than one gram of **mass** transformed into pure energy to destroy the Japanese city of Hiroshima at the end of World War II. Looking out to a safer distance in outer space, astronomers and astrophysicists regularly see signs of energy converting into matter and back again—what they call "annihilation radiation" from, among other places, the center of our galaxy. In this case, high-energy particles of light, or **photons,** can turn into another particle, called an **electron,** and its **antimatter**

Figure 1.1 In 1945, when an atomic bomb was dropped on Hiroshima, Japan by U.S. forces smoke billowed 20,000 feet (6 km) above the city.

partner, an anti-electron, which is also known as a **positron**. The matter and antimatter particles then collide and destroy each other, releasing energy that can be detected from across the galaxy. Matter and energy are truly interchangeable, and evidence of this appears in both the heavens and the history books.

Einstein also showed that energy actually has some weight. A fully charged battery, for example, will weigh ever so slightly more than one that's gone dead (even though this extra weight is far too small to feel). Even more surprising, scientists in the last century have discovered that much of the matter in the universe cannot be seen. This **dark matter** seems to outweigh "normal" matter by

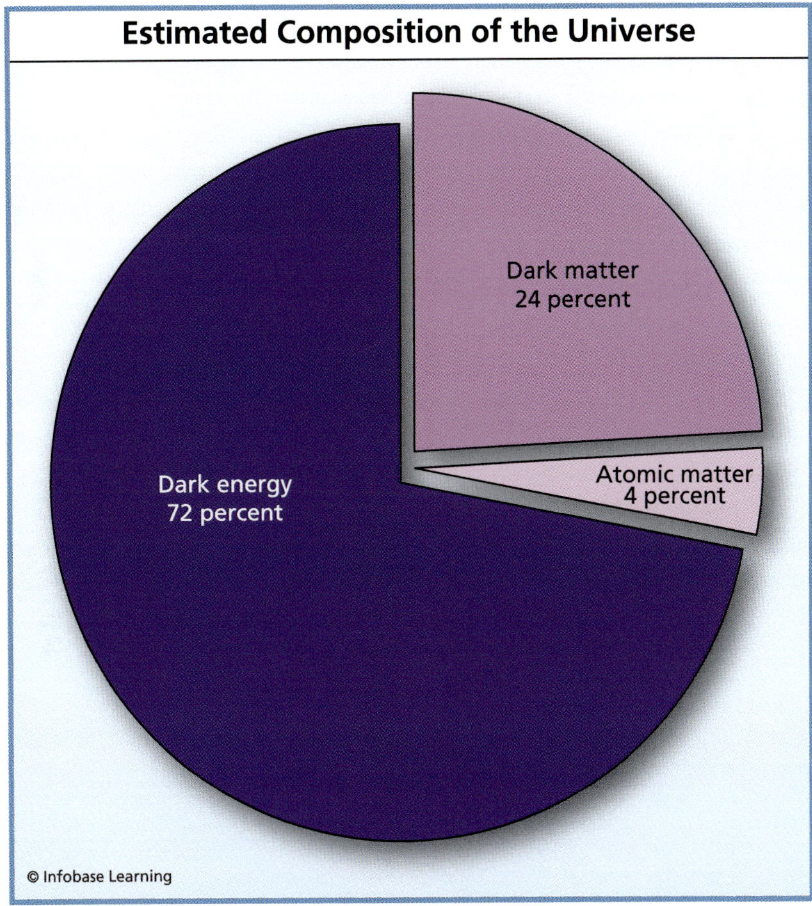

Figure 1.2   Today, scientists believe that all of the atoms that make up living beings, planets, stars, and galaxies provide only 4% of the total matter and energy in the universe. Dark matter, considered an unknown type of subatomic particle, accounts for another 24%. All the rest is dark energy, a mysterious force that opposes gravity.

a considerable margin. Furthermore, it was only in the late 1990s when scientists realized the great majority of the universe seems to be composed of even more exotic **dark energy**. Scientists are only beginning to learn about dark energy, but its properties may determine the fate of the universe.

The first three chapters of *Matter and Energy* will explain what matter and energy are and how they work, beginning with the concepts of classical physics, from the various forms of energy—such as the energy of motion and the energy of gravity, to the concepts of matter—weight, mass, and the wide variety of particles in nature. Chapter 4 explores Einstein's insights about the interchangeability of matter and energy, and how this concept is now used both for practical purposes, such as making electricity in power plants, and to help understand the universe. Finally, Chapters 5 and 6 look at how matter and energy play off of each other throughout the entire universe. "Dark matter" and "dark energy" make up the majority of the universe, and they will help determine the ultimate fate of the cosmos. The remaining chapters will show how they were first discovered, how astronomers and **cosmologists** are using them to help understand the universe better, and why they are important in understanding how the universe might end billions of years from now.

Amazingly, the basic concepts of matter and energy describe very small things such as subatomic particles as well as the behavior of very large things such as black holes and clusters of galaxies. With the entire universe as a canvas, it's time to start filling in the details.

2

What Matter Is

Chances are that, as you read, you are sitting in a chair and breathing air. You may have recently had a glass of water or milk, or maybe eaten a snack. Later in the day, you may watch a program on a plasma-screen television. Every minute of every day, you are coming in contact with matter, in its many forms. Anything you can hold contains matter, and all matter is, in turn, made of atoms and **molecules**, or even smaller parts. After learning the secrets of matter, you will understand the world in a new and deeper way.

ATOMS AND MOLECULES

Picture a brick wall and think about how it was built. A bricklayer sat or knelt, holding a trowel in one hand and a brick in another, and repeatedly put down a layer of mortar and set a brick in just the right place to construct this strong wall. Mortar and brick, mortar and brick, mortar and brick, layer after layer after layer until the wall was finished. When the bricklayer reached the end and the mortar dried, the wall was built. However, this is usually not the end of the process: Houses, schools, and other buildings are made of a number of walls, arranged in a pattern that forms rooms and hallways. In fact, if the bricklayer is following a master plan, he will build many walls to put together a useful structure. On its own, every brick is

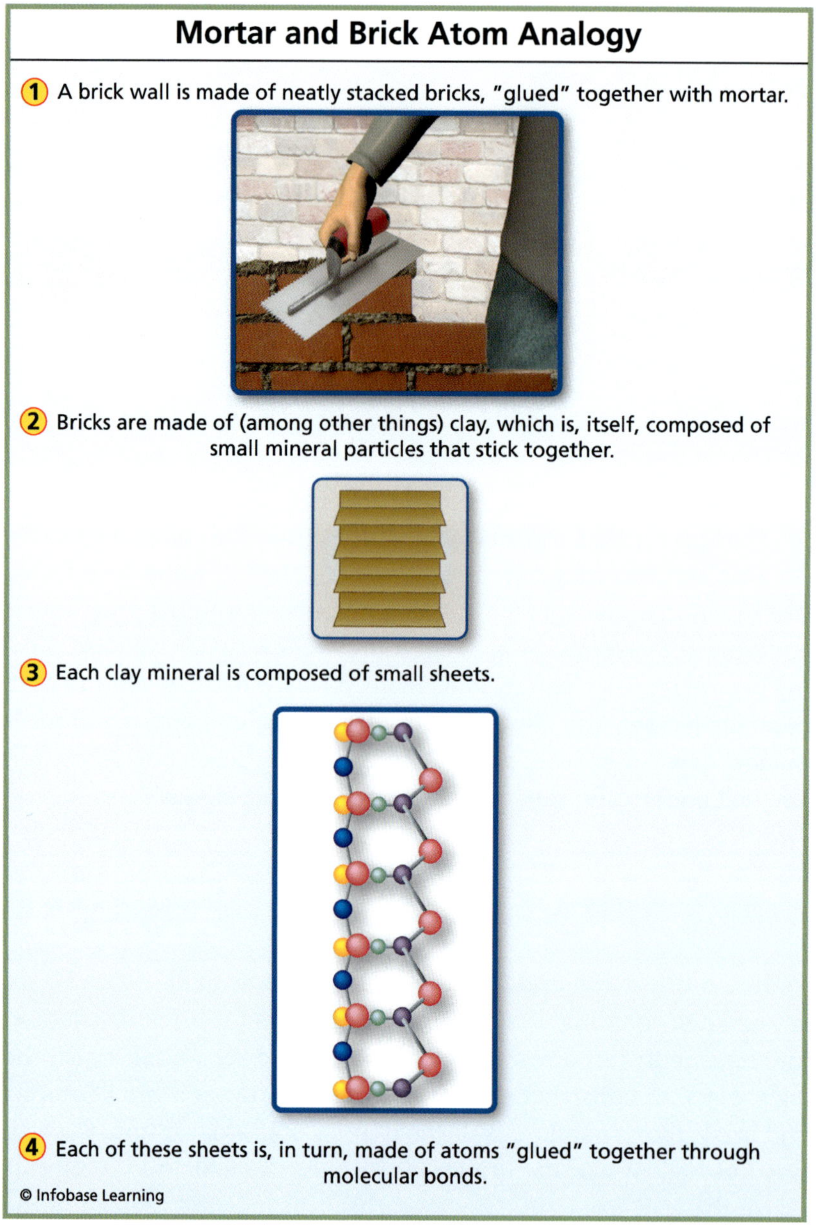
Mortar and Brick Atom Analogy
1 A brick wall is made of neatly stacked bricks, "glued" together with mortar.
2 Bricks are made of (among other things) clay, which is, itself, composed of small mineral particles that stick together.
3 Each clay mineral is composed of small sheets.
4 Each of these sheets is, in turn, made of atoms "glued" together through molecular bonds.
© Infobase Learning

Figure 2.1 The structure of atoms can be likened to bricks and mortar.

simple: a brick-shaped chunk of clay. Yet simple building blocks can be assembled into something as complex as a school, provided the bricklayer is careful to follow the plans he is given.

Now imagine picking up a brick and looking under a microscope. The brick is made primarily of clay, so what shows up under the microscope is a profusion of small, flat masses of clay particles. Clay particles tend to be very tiny (no more than a few millionths of a meter, or microns, in size) and are usually flat and shaped like dinner plates. In the brick, they look sort of like a pile of Frisbees: not stacked up neatly, but not randomly placed either. Most of the clay particles will be lying more or less flat and overlapping each other. It is this overlap that gives strength to the clay, just as the overlap of bricks in each adjacent row lends strength to the wall. All of these tiny clay particles are the building blocks of each brick, just as the bricks are the blocks from which a school is built.

This can be taken even further. It is possible to examine a single clay particle with a high-powered microscope. Even a single, two-micron clay particle turns out to be remarkably complicated when looked at closely enough. Every particle of clay turns out to be composed of tiny sheets, like the sheets of paper that make up this book. Furthermore, looking even more closely, each of these sheets turns out to be built of even smaller building blocks: These building blocks are the atoms.

In the example here, the atoms are the building blocks of molecules (the sheets that make up the clay minerals), molecules are the building blocks of clay particles, clay particles are the building blocks of bricks, and bricks are the building blocks of house and school walls. And, as walls can be arranged in any number of ways to form different buildings, atoms can be arranged in any number of patterns to form different molecules, and molecules can take on any number of arrangements to form different materials. Thus, carbon atoms might be arranged in sheets to form the soft graphite in a pencil lead, arranged in a rigid cage to form a hard diamond, or they might be mixed with oxygen to form the carbon dioxide that we exhale with every breath.

Another example is water. Water is made of two hydrogen (H) atoms connected to an oxygen (O) atom. These three atoms together form a molecule, called H_2O. Seen under a microscope, a single water molecule looks like a mouse's head: the oxygen atom is the face, and the two smaller hydrogen atoms are the ears!

MASS

Atoms are incredibly light, and they are also incredibly small. It takes billions upon billions of atoms to make even the smallest of visible objects. (For example, the period at the end of this sentence is a few million atoms wide.) Atoms are very light, but put enough of them together and they add up to something with a weight that can be easily detected. The amount of matter in an object is its mass. The more mass something has, the harder it will be to push, and the heavier it will be in Earth's gravity. Mass is one of the fundamental properties of matter, and scientists are still trying to understand it more fully. Here is what they know, as well as what they suspect might be the case.

Why Is There Any Matter in the Universe?

At the moment of the Big Bang, the universe was almost certainly composed entirely of energy. As the universe began to cool, matter began to form—as did antimatter. In fact, according to standard theories of physics, matter *and* antimatter should both have been formed in equal quantities—just as, in pair production, an electron and a positron are both formed. This is an example of what is called symmetry. Yet had this been the case, there would currently be nothing in the universe at all—all matter and antimatter would have annihilated each other, leaving the universe with only energy. The best guess today is that, for some unknown reason, there was a very slight imbalance or asymmetry in the formation of matter and antimatter— for every 10 billion atoms of antimatter formed, there were 10 billion and one atoms of matter. This very slight excess of matter may account for how it became possible for our planet, the solar system—in fact, just about everything we can see in the universe—to form. Still, nobody yet knows exactly why there was this asymmetry—why matter and antimatter didn't just cancel each other out. The reason why we exist at all remains a deep mystery.

The mass of atoms is measured in units called **atomic mass units** (amu). The lightest atom, the hydrogen atom, has a mass of 1.01 amu. One gram (about the mass of a single packet of sugar) weighs about 6.022×10^{23} amu. This number would be written out as 602,200,000,000,000,000,000,000 and is equal to the mass of roughly 600 thousand billion billion hydrogen atoms. This means that this number of hydrogen atoms is needed to make a gram of hydrogen atoms, which is the mass of a packet of sugar.

An atom is made up of even smaller parts: a hard core called a **nucleus**, surrounded by light particles called electrons, which fly around the nucleus like bees around a hive. The nucleus, in turn, is made of particles called **protons** and **neutrons**. Protons are positively charged particles; neutrons have zero electric charge.

Hydrogen is the simplest atom. In its most common form, hydrogen is made of a single proton surrounded by a single electron. Most atoms are made of various numbers of protons, neutrons, and electrons. Oxygen, for example, is made of a nucleus of 8 protons and 8 neutrons surrounded by 8 electrons. An iron atom is composed of 26 protons and 30 neutrons surrounded by 26 electrons. An atom of lead is pretty heavy as atoms go: Its 82 electrons surround a nucleus made of 82 protons and as many as 126 neutrons. So, 1 gram is the mass of 6.022×10^{23} hydrogen atoms, or 2.9×10^{21} (2.9 billion trillion) atoms of lead.

All of this helps explain why agglomerations of atoms have mass: They are just collections of protons and neutrons, but it does not explain why protons and neutrons should weigh anything, or why they each weigh about 2,000 times as much as an electron. Unless science can explain why each proton and neutron has mass, why each electron has much less mass, and why photons (particles of light) weigh nothing at all, it cannot explain why even such a simple, everyday object (such as a book) has the particular value of mass that it does.

Enter Higgs!

In 2009, CERN, also known as the European Organization for Nuclear Research, launched a huge multinational particle accelerator—known as the Large Hadron Collider (LHC)—designed to smash protons into each other at nearly the speed of light. If scientists see what they expect, one of these collisions will very briefly form a state of matter that has not been seen in our part of the universe for nearly

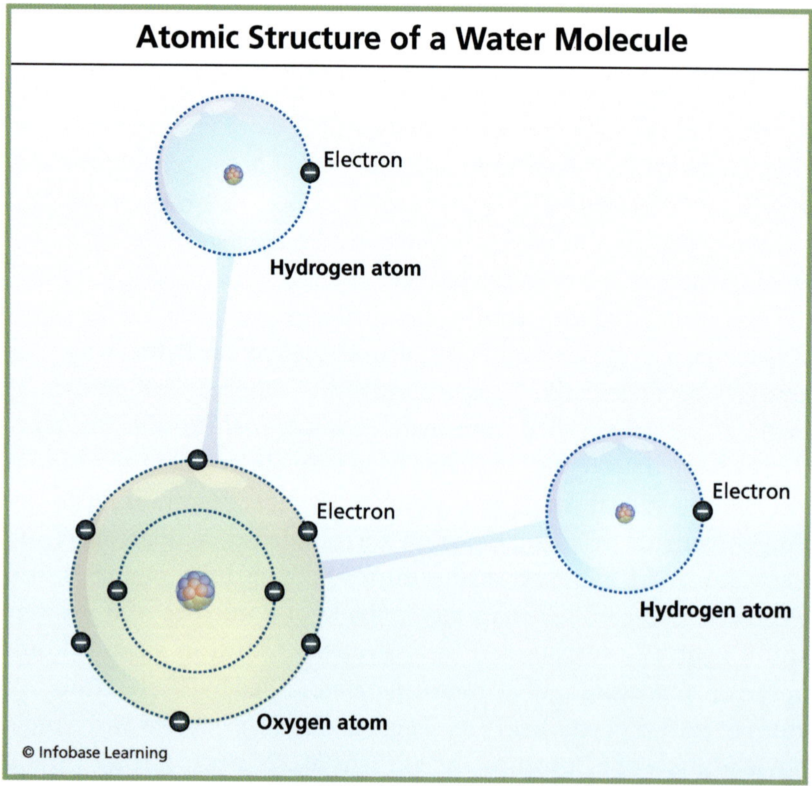

Figure 2.2   If you could see inside each atom, a water molecule would look like this.

14 billion years when it was only a fraction of a second old. How does this event relate to the issue of mass?

The particle that scientists hope to see, called the **Higgs particle** (after Peter Higgs, the physicist who first suggested it might exist), is one that they suspect gives everything its mass. According to Higgs, all of space is filled with a field, just as a bathtub may be filled with water, and this field can be explained by the Higgs particle. Particles moving through space have no choice but to interact with the Higgs field, just as any object passing through water has no choice but to make waves. However, not every object interacts the same way with the field. For example, it is easier to wave a knife through the water than a sheet of plywood. Using this analogy, the more "drag" is felt, the more a particle weighs. An electron would

Figure 2.3   Peter Higgs is pictured in April 2008, while visiting the CMS experiment at CERN's Large Hadron Collider, which is seeking to find the elusive Higgs boson—a hypothetical, massive elementary particle predicted to exist by the Standard Model of particle physics.

be like the knife blade, slicing through the Higgs field with only a little interaction, while protons and neutrons are like the plywood. Photons skimming the surface of the water would weigh nothing at all. If science is successful in discovering the Higgs particle, it may be able to explain why individual protons and neutrons weigh what they do, explaining in turn why every kind of object in the universe has a specific mass.

SIZE

An official major-league baseball is about 2.9 inches (7.4 centimeters) in diameter. Human hairs are about 18 to 180 microns (millionths of a meter) in width. A Boeing 747-400 is about 231 feet long (70.4 meters), Earth is about 24,000 miles (38,624 kilometers) around, and so on. One of the ways to describe things is by their size. Why objects have certain sizes is not as big a mystery as why they have the mass they do, but it is important and, in some respects, even astonishing.

The short version of why everything has size is that everything is made of atoms, and atoms have sizes. A carbon atom, for example, has a size of about 70 picometers (pm). (A picometer is equal to a millionth of a millionth of a meter.) So, if it were possible to line up carbon atoms single file, it would take more than 14 million of them to make a line about 0.03 inches (1 millimeter) long. Since there are about 25 mm in one inch, there would be about 363 million carbon atoms in an inch. However, it's not *quite* that simple, mainly because atoms don't normally line up nicely right next to each other.

Picture a group of students standing in a classroom. Say each student measures about six inches (150 mm) from front to back and is about 1.5 feet (457 mm) shoulder to shoulder. If the goal is to cram all of them into the smallest space possible, then a class of 20 students would fit into a line only 10 feet (3 m) long; or all of the kids could be crammed into a corner in a mass that would be about 5 feet (1.5 m) long and 3 feet (0.9 m) wide. However, this degree of packing would mean that everyone would be touching everyone else, standing on each other's feet, and smelling each other's breath. People don't like to stand so close together; they like to have some space. This is why a line of 20 students will be 20 or 30 feet (6 or 9 m) long, or even longer. This is also why a classroom for 20 students is so large: Every student needs to have some space around them. So, in reality, while it is possible to cram everyone into a small corner, this is never done.

By the same token, atoms don't like to be crammed together. Each atom also needs its space. In diamonds, the carbon atoms tend to stay about 154 picometers apart from each other. So, a 1 mm diamond crystal would hold about 6.5 million carbon atoms, not the more than 14 million atoms calculated earlier. Incidentally, carbon atoms don't always stay at the same distance. For example, in a sheet of graphite (one of the components of the "lead" in a pencil), carbon atoms tend to stay a little closer (about 142 pm). Therefore, a few more carbon atoms are lined up in 0.03-inch (1 mm) piece of graphite, which amounts to about 7 million carbon atoms. What this all means is that it is not only the size of an atom, but also the distance it keeps from its neighbors that determine the size of a cluster of atoms. And, of these two factors, it is the "personal space" that each

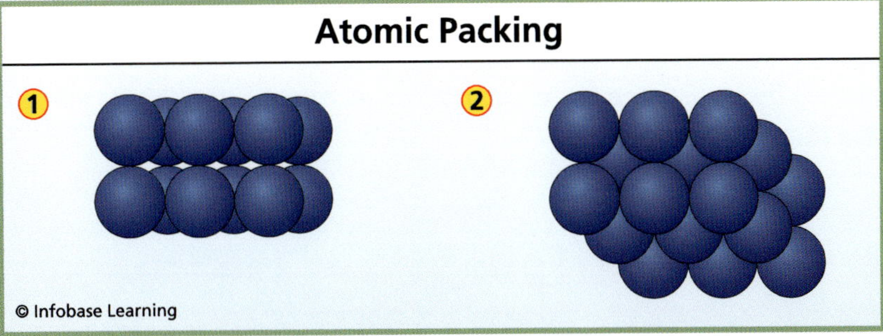

Figure 2.4 This diagram provides an example of how atoms can be packed together. (1) Stacking balls, or atoms, directly on top of each other forms straight columns, but there are a lot of unused spaces between each one. (2) Placing the balls of one layer in the unused space of the lower layer results in denser packing.

atom needs that is most important. Like people, atoms themselves aren't all that large. The most important factor in determining the size of a collection of atoms is the distance that each atom likes to keep from its neighbors.

Believe it or not, things are a little more interesting when we take an even closer look. It turns out that even the size of an atom is sort of misleading. A hydrogen atom is about 25 picometers in size. Hydrogen's nucleus contains a single proton, which is about one ten-thousandth the size of the entire atom, at a little less than two femtometers (millionths of a billionth of a meter) in size. What all of these numbers mean is that virtually all of the mass in an atom occupies a very tiny space in the center. The nucleus is surrounded by a huge empty space containing just a single electron at the atom's outermost edge. Think, for example, of a single fly buzzing around in the center of a domed football stadium and you have an idea of how much empty space is inside an atom. In the house example, all of the mass of the house is in the bricks that make up the walls, but the walls enclose a lot of empty space. It might be possible to stack up all of the bricks that make up a house in a single room. However, it is both the way that the bricks are arranged and the size of the space that they enclose that makes the house as large as it is, just as it is the distance that the electrons keep from the central nucleus that makes atoms as large as they are.

Thus, this combination of factors—that atoms are so much larger than the nuclei (where almost all of the mass is) and that they like to keep their distance from each other—explains why things are the size that they are.

STATES OF MATTER: SOLID, LIQUID, GAS, PLASMA, AND LIQUID CRYSTAL

Open the freezer, take out an ice cube, and put it on the counter. Pretty soon it will start to melt. Eventually, a puddle of water will form where the ice cube used to be. Leave it overnight and, in the morning, the water will have evaporated. Or put the ice cube in a pan on the stove and turn on the heat. Now, the melting and evaporation happens even more quickly. This is something that happens every day. It is such an unremarkable occurrence that very few people even think about it. Yet, if you think about it a little more, it becomes a little more interesting.

Matter comes in several states: **Solid, liquid**, and **gas** are the best known. These are the three states that the ice cube went through as it melted: the solid ice became liquid water, which then became the gas known as water vapor. Again, this process is so common that it is taken for granted. However, think about it: How many other solids will melt at room temperature? How many liquids will turn into vapor at room temperature all by themselves? The opposite process also happens when dew forms or a mirror steams up: vapor becomes liquid. How many vapors will turn back into liquids before our eyes? In fact, water is one of the few compounds that changes from one state to another so safely and easily.

Melting ice doesn't sound very impressive, but things get more interesting at the atomic and molecular level. Ice is made of water molecules, each of which is locked into place, like cars in a traffic jam. In a heavy traffic jam, it's hard to imagine that one car can instantly change places with a car five rows in front of it. Atoms and molecules in a solid are like this too, each in its assigned place, and each unlikely to move on its own.

When a solid begins to heat up, the atoms start to vibrate and jump and, when it gets hot enough, they will vibrate strongly enough

Figure 2.5   This image of Mendenhall Lake and Glacier in Juneau, Alaska, shows the three phases of water—solid ice, liquid ocean, and vapor clouds.

that they can start to jump out of their assigned places. This is what happens when something like an ice cube melts. When traffic starts to flow again, each car can switch lanes and change its position, like a smoothly flowing liquid. When traffic begins to open up completely, cars are free to move to any lane they want and other cars move away from them. This is like a gas. If a solid is heated up enough, the atoms begin to jump out of their assigned locations and mix together in a puddle of liquid. If the liquid is heated still more, the atoms and molecules will vibrate and jump with so much energy that they can't even hold together in a liquid. They then become a gas.

This process—changing from one state of matter to another—is called a **phase transition**, and phase transitions are important in physics. In phase transitions, atoms are becoming either less organized or more organized, and the property of the matter changes

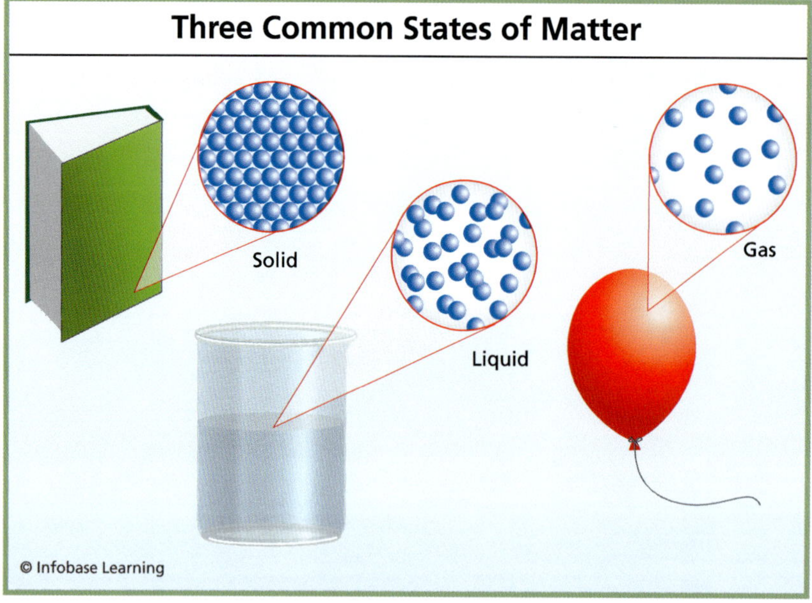

Figure 2.6 The particles within a solid are packed more closely together than particles in a liquid or gas.

from solid to liquid, or from liquid to solid. In the example of the traffic jam, the cars underwent a "phase transition" from being locked in place to moving freely. It is relatively easy to change phase in the other direction: cooling steam forms water, and cooling water forms ice.

Solids, liquids, and gases are well known, but scientists have also identified many other states of matter. Two examples are liquid crystals and **plasmas**. Liquid crystals have some properties that resemble solids, and some properties that are more liquid, but they really are neither of these. Liquid crystals were considered sort of odd when they were first discovered, but they are now used in calculators, watches, computer monitors, and thin-screen television sets.

A plasma is a gas made up of charged particles. Remember that atoms are formed of a nucleus surrounded by a cloud of electrons, and the number of electrons is equal to the number of protons. If one electron is removed, there is now a positively charged atom (called an ion) and a negatively charged electron. Plasmas are all gases,

Figure 2.7   When plasma from the Sun slams into Earth's magnetic field, Northern Lights, such as these in Norway, are naturally produced.

but their electrical charge makes them different from air and other gases. Plasmas are found all over the universe. The Sun is a plasma of hot charged gas, as are all stars. The beautiful, glowing clouds of gas that are seen in photos from the Hubble Space Telescope are plasmas. However, plasmas also abound on Earth. The inside of a compact fluorescent light bulb is also a plasma, for example, as are some television screens, the glow of a lightning bolt, and the colors of the Northern Lights. In fact, even though plasmas are not nearly as familiar to us as solids, liquids, and gases, they are the most common state of matter in the universe.

3

What Energy Is

Energy crisis. Solar energy. **Nuclear energy, solar energy, geothermal energy**, and **wind energy**. Energy is in the news every day and is a constant topic of discussion. Since everyone talks about energy, one would think that everyone must know exactly what it is, right? Well, it turns out that not everyone knows exactly what energy is. Or maybe a better way to put it is that scientists have a very precise definition of what energy is and this definition is different from what most people mean when they talk about energy on the news. So it's a good idea to start with trying to figure out exactly what scientists mean when they use the word *energy*, and how their usage compares to the way that most people use the term, and then go on from there.

According to *Merriam-Webster's Collegiate Dictionary*, energy is "a fundamental entity of nature that is transferred between parts of a system in the production of physical change within the system and usually regarded as the capacity for doing work." That is all that energy is: the capacity to do work. Scientists also talk about the **conservation of energy**—meaning that energy can neither be created nor destroyed. When a portable music player is turned on, the **chemical energy** of its battery does some useful work: The battery's energy is converted into the **electrical energy** that lights up the display screen and transmits a signal containing the music. (In addition, some **heat energy** gets created in the process, too.) Then, the electrical signal gets converted into sound energy as it reaches

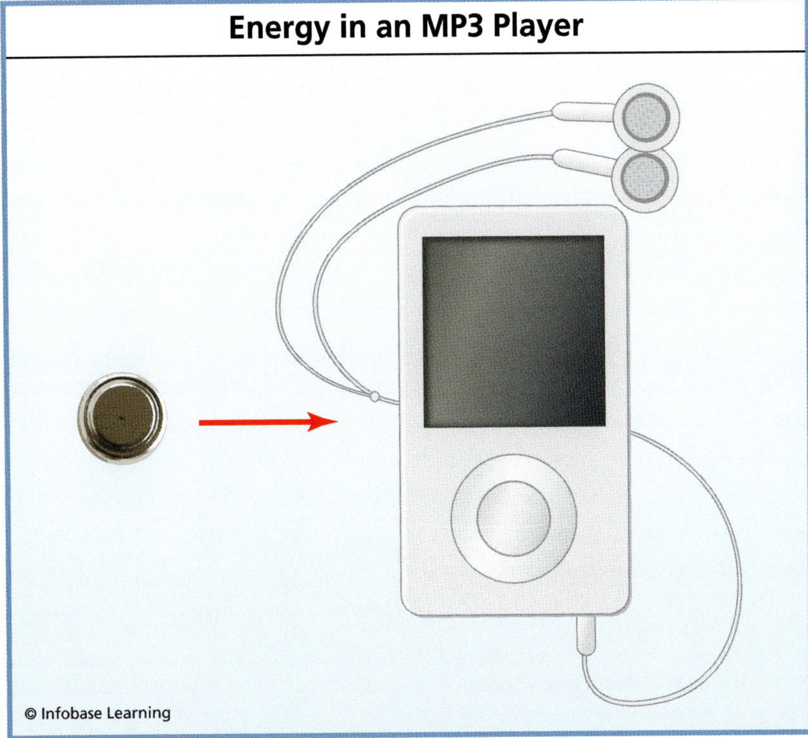

Figure 3.1 Chemical energy in a battery turns into electrical energy to run an MP3 player. Inside the player, the electrical energy turns into the rotational energy of the hard drive, as well as visible light from the screen and acoustic energy from the earbuds.

a listener's earphones. None of that energy from the battery really disappears—it just turns into other forms.

When energy is mentioned on the news, people are usually talking about *sources* of stored energy that can be converted into such useful work as powering a car or turning on a computer. They are typically not talking about the energy itself, or how it never gets actually created or destroyed. Instead, they are usually talking about a source of energy, such as coal or petroleum or sunlight that can be transformed into something that performs useful work.

Nuclear power is a *source* of energy; it is a way to help people to do work. A nuclear reactor produces heat, which raises the temperature of water. The hot water turns to steam, which turns a turbine, which generates electricity that can then be sent to power homes.

So think about this process and remember that energy itself is a measure of a system's capacity to do useful work. In a nuclear power plant, this work consists of turning a turbine. The uranium atoms in the nuclear reactor can't do any work; by themselves, they are unable to turn a turbine to produce electricity. Cold water is also unable to turn an electrical turbine. So, in a nuclear power plant, neither uranium atoms nor water alone can do the work of producing electricity. However, the uranium atoms are what make it possible to do this work. Energy is stored within the uranium atoms, and when these atoms split apart, that energy is released and it heats up the water. The heated water contains the energy to make steam, and the steam causes the turbine to turn. Thus, the energy stored in the uranium atoms is what makes it possible for the turbines to do work after that energy is released.

This sort of process can be performed with any sort of energy. Consider, for example, petroleum, which produces gasoline. Petroleum in and of itself is simply a liquid, usually gooey and black. For most of history, it was not considered a source of energy. In fact, until the late 1800s, petroleum was more likely to be used for lubrication or as a medicine, or maybe to light a lamp, than it was to be burned to create energy. However, people then realized they could refine (meaning to remove less useful substances from) the black goo. Before it is refined and burned, petroleum is simply a sticky, stinking liquid, but when that black goo is processed to make gasoline, the gasoline is then sprayed into an engine cylinder and lit. The resulting explosion pushes a piston, which turns a camshaft and makes it possible to drive a car or truck. Once it was realized that petroleum could be refined and burned, and that this burning could make it possible to accomplish work, petroleum became a source of energy—but not until that point.

Let's now consider water as a source of energy. It sounds slightly silly to put water into the same category as petroleum, mainly because fresh water doesn't burn. On the other hand, the Hoover Dam in Nevada uses water to drive turbines. In other words, the water behind the dam has the ability to perform work. Thus, obviously there is energy of a sort in water, if only in its ability to turn turbines as it falls. This energy comes from gravity. Drop a ball out

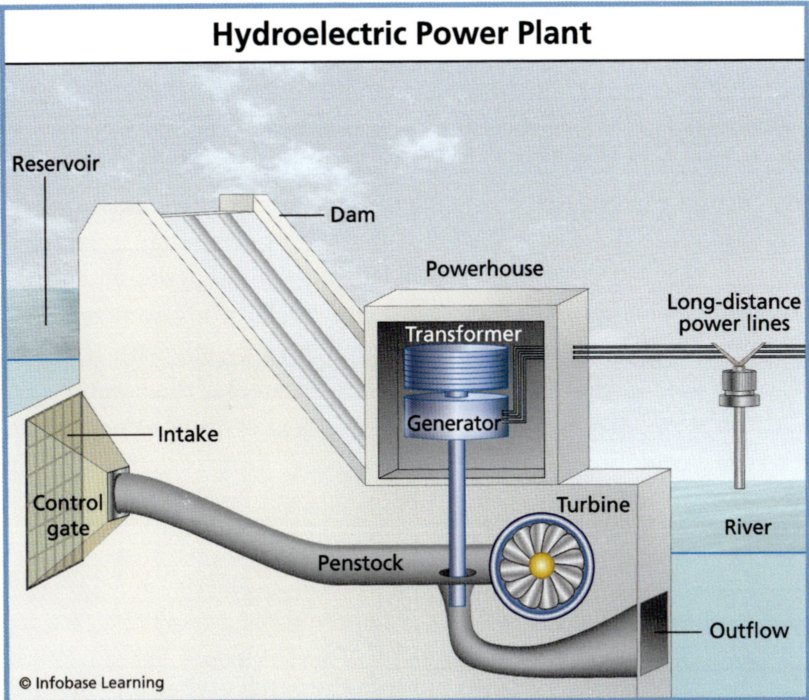

Figure 3.2 A hydroelectric power plant collects energy found in moving water and converts it into electricity.

of a window and it gains a lot of energy as it reaches the ground. At the top of the dam, water contains a lot of energy because of gravity's pull—and this **potential energy** is released as it falls to the bottom of the dam.

Water also stores other kinds of energy. Water is comprised of three atoms, one oxygen and two hydrogen, and hydrogen can burn. So hydrogen, when removed from the rest of a water molecule, can be a source of chemical energy. However, it takes some energy to split up a water molecule and obtain this hydrogen. Still, scientists and engineers are interested in creating vehicles that use the hydrogen as a fuel. Although a power plant would have to spend energy to release hydrogen from water or other molecules, hydrogen-powered vehicles would not produce pollution on the road. In fact, burned hydrogen fuel would combine with oxygen to produce clean water in the exhaust.

More ambitiously, scientists and engineers are learning to use hydrogen to power a fusion reactor, which could potentially release far more energy than it needs to operate. In fusion power, the cores of hydrogen atoms, or their nuclei, are smashed together, a process that releases a lot of energy. Experimental fusion reactors exist, but the current reactors have a problem—it takes as much or more energy to create the fusion reaction than the power that is released through the fusion of nuclei. Still, fusion produces a tremendous amount of energy when two hydrogen nuclei are fused together, and there is the potential to make it much more efficient. If fusion reactors ever become practical sources of energy, then water may become as important to the world of the next century as petroleum is to the world today.

STORED ENERGY

Energy can be stored in many ways. For example, a battery stores chemical energy. The energy is put into the battery when it is charged and, as the energy is released, it powers whatever the battery happens to be attached to. The chemical energy stored within a car's battery, for example, does the work of turning the starter motor and firing the spark plugs when a car is starting up. So batteries are one way of storing energy.

There are many mechanical ways to store energy (stored mechanical energy is also called potential energy). Compressing a spring stores energy, which is released when the spring is released. This is what powers many watches and clocks: Winding up a clock tightens a spring, storing energy that is released over the period of a day or longer. Stored energy also helps raise garage doors and elevators; garage doors have large springs that are stretching as the door drops so that the stored energy can help the relatively tiny motor raise the heavy door when it is time to open it up again. With elevators, energy is stored in counterweights attached to the elevator by long cables. When the elevator is on the ground floor, the counterweights are near the top of the building, from where they exert an upward pull on the elevator. As the elevator rises, the stored energy in the weights helps the motor pull the elevator car upward.

A reservoir is another way of storing energy, and this is part of how Hoover Dam works. The dam traps water behind it (the water

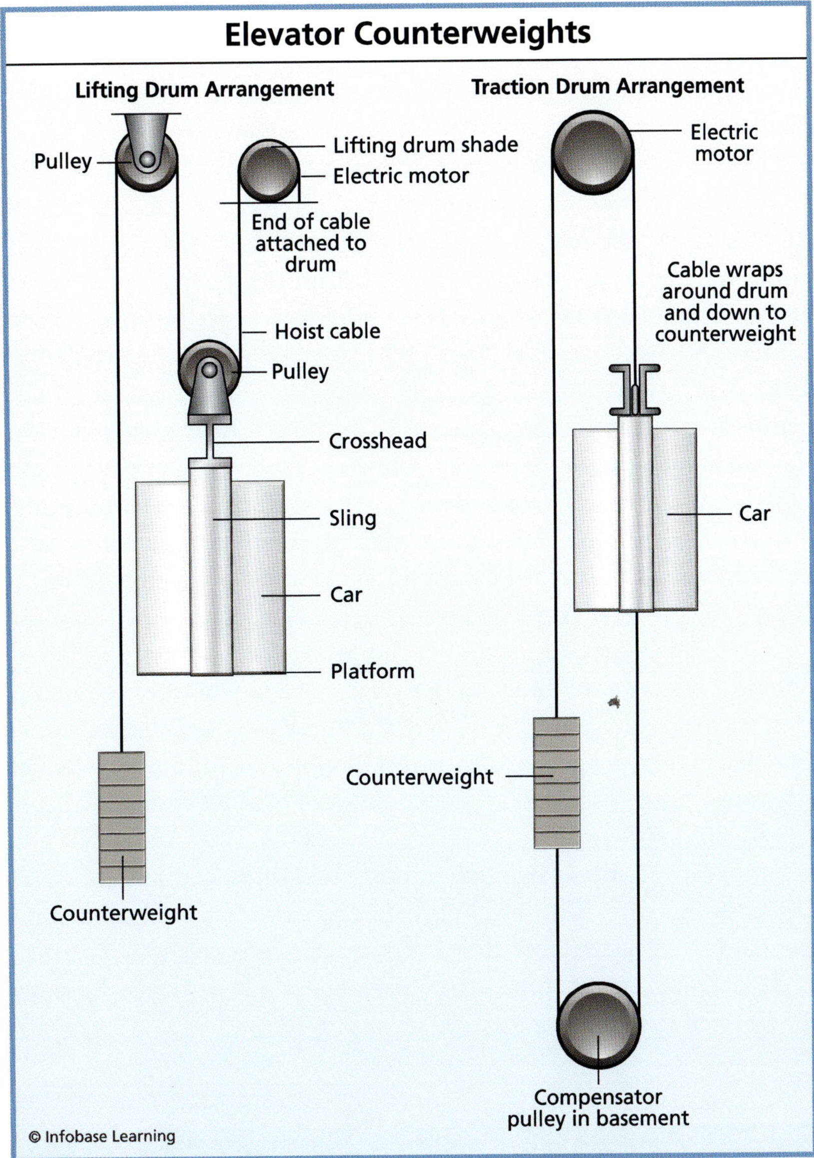

Figure 3.3 An elevator's system of cables and counterweights enables it to move the elevator car up and down.

level is more than 700 feet [213 m] higher on the upstream side of the dam than it is on the downstream side). The water behind the dam represents stored energy because when the water is allowed to flow through a turbine, the energy stored by gravity is released as it falls, picking up speed. The energy of its motion (**kinetic energy**) does the work of turning a turbine to generate electricity. This makes the reservoir behind a dam another way to store energy.

In fact, there are an incredible number of ways that energy can be stored. For example, gasoline is also full of chemical energy, but this energy is not released until the gasoline is burned. Until that point, the chemical energy is stored within the gasoline molecules, just waiting for a spark to set it free to do work. Every uranium atom contains stored energy, as does every hydrogen atom; in fact, a hydrogen atom can release different amounts of stored energy, depending on what will be done to it. Burning a hydrogen atom releases a small amount of energy (a few electron volts), while joining together the cores of two hydrogen atoms—fusion—releases a few million electron volts of energy. And this is another important point: The amount of energy that something can release may be different depending on what type of energy is being extracted from it. Simple technologies (a dam, for example) can extract only the gravity-based potential energy contained in falling water. More complex technologies, such as hydrogen-powered cars, can release the chemical energy of burning hydrogen, and the most complex technologies—fusion reactors—can release the far greater amount of nuclear energy that is stored within the nuclei of the hydrogen atoms. This means that one cannot really know how much energy something can release without knowing what kind of energy will be extracted and used. And the kind of stored energy that is extracted—whether gravitational, chemical, nuclear, or some other form—depends on the technology that is used to liberate it.

ENERGY FIELDS

Anyone who is familiar with science fiction is probably familiar with energy fields. What many science fiction fans may not realize is that energy fields exist today, and they can do work, as well. However, what they are and how they work is not always easy to understand when we move from the world of science fiction to science fact. Therefore, a few examples may be in order.

First, however, there is a sort of confession to make: Many physicists use the term *field* to describe things like gravity, magnetism, and energy. However, they really don't like using this word. To many physicists, talking about *fields* is a sort of a cop-out: To them it means that they are not explaining the smallest details about what is happening. Many physicists will say that energy fields don't really exist. Fields are just a useful concept but are not helpful for getting a deeper and more advanced description of the basic physics. In fact, many energy *fields* can now be understood as really consisting of particles being exchanged in very complicated ways. Nevertheless, fields are a useful starting point for understanding questions related to energy. With that in mind, here are some examples of how energy fields can perform work.

Some of the most visible features of our Sun are sunspots, the dark spots that freckle the face of our nearest star. In the early seventeenth century, the Italian scientist Galileo Galilei was amazed to see blemishes on what most of his contemporaries believed to be a perfect object. Several centuries later, astronomers found that sunspots are places where the Sun's magnetic field loops out from it. Further studies found that this magnetic field can become twisted up inside the Sun, like a rubber band that is used to power a model airplane or a toy car. As the Sun rotates, these magnetic field lines twist and kink, storing energy in the solar magnetic field. Twist a rubber band enough and it will break, snapping against your fingers and sometimes causing a bit of pain as it releases the energy that was stored by the twisting. Twist a magnetic field enough and it, too, will break. However, when a magnetic field on an object that is as large as the Sun breaks, a lot more energy is released. When the solar magnetic field lines break and reconnect, massive amounts of hydrogen and helium are spewed into space. Any astronaut who is exposed, unshielded, to one of these solar storms would surely die from this fast-flying hydrogen and helium radiation. When a storm such as this hits Earth, it can destroy satellites and can even knock out cell phone networks or electrical power systems across a large chunk of a continent. So, this is one form of an energy field—the energy that is stored in a magnetic field when it is twisted up by the rotation of a star.

The Sun is not the only star to store massive amounts of energy in a magnetic field, by the way. Astronomers have observed

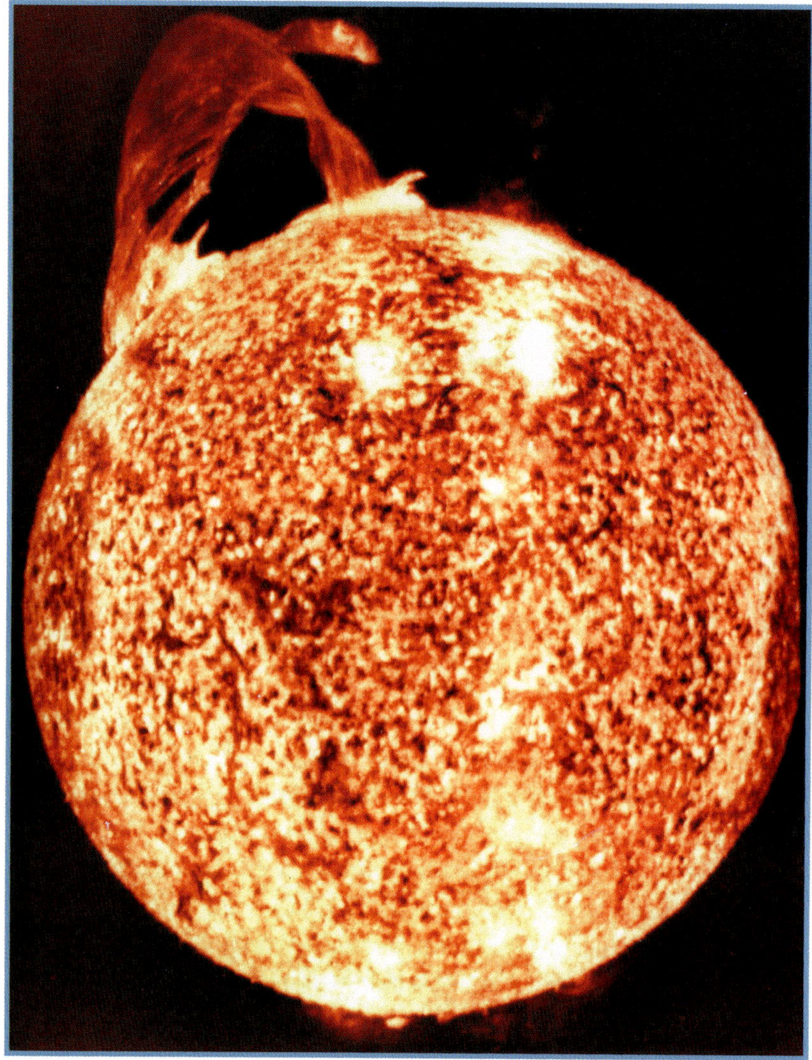

Figure 3.4 This image captures one of the most spectacular solar flares ever recorded, spanning more than 365,366 miles (588,000 km) across the solar surface.

strong magnetic fields around black holes and neutron stars. Those with the strongest magnetic fields are called *magnetars* (for magnetic stars). In 2004, a magnetar in the Milky Way galaxy (about

50,000 light-years from Earth) released an incredible amount of stored magnetic field energy that reached our planet. The resulting burst of radiation, even from so great a distance, was enough to measurably raise radiation dose rates in space. Astronauts in space would have received about as much radiation from this magnetar as they would receive from a dental X-ray. Other strong magnetic fields (with large amounts of stored energy) have been observed virtually everywhere in the universe that has been observed by astronomers.

Another form of energy field is a little closer to Earth: electrical generators and motors. Both of these make use of the fact that electricity and magnetism are really two aspects of the same thing: Magnetism can be used to generate electricity, and electricity can be used to induce magnetism. It is the electric and magnetic fields that make this transformation possible. In a generator, for example, an electrical conductor (such as a loop of wire) rotates around a magnetic field. This movement around a magnetic field causes electricity to flow through the wire, generating electricity. It really doesn't matter if the wire is rotating within the magnetic field, or if the magnetic field is rotating around the wire. All that matters is that there is motion between the two. When the magnetic field moves past the conductor, it exerts forces on electrons in the conductor (the wire). These now-moving electrons create a current that is then able to perform the work of turning an electric motor, powering a computer, and so forth.

What these "fields" have in common is that there is no real physical connection between the object that is generating the field and the object that is absorbing the energy. In an engine, for example, the gasoline is ignited and the explosion forces a piston to move. In a nuclear reactor, the fissioning uranium atom heats the reactor fuel, which heats the water, which turns a turbine. In both of these examples—and in countless others—there is a direct physical connection between the source of energy and the work that is being performed. This is not the case with energy fields: A magnetic field is not a physical object, and there is no direct physical connection between the magnetic field and the wires in an electric generator. What is really happening is that there is an exchange of photons— particles of light—between the object generating the magnetism and the wires in an electric generator. However, it's simpler to first use magnetic fields to describe this setup.

RADIATION

Yet another form of energy is **radiation**. In science, radiation takes on a somewhat broader meaning than it does on news programs, when it's usually mentioned in connection with medical procedures or nuclear exposure. In science, radiation is the transfer of any sort of energy or particle from one place to another, such as from the Sun to Earth.

Antimatter

Anyone who watches *Star Trek*, and likely anyone familiar with any sort of science fiction, will be familiar with antimatter, though that familiarity may stop with the word itself. However, antimatter may be the most potent form of energy in the universe, if enough of it can be made and harnessed.

Matter is what makes up most of the everyday world: Earth, the Sun, rocks, cars, and so forth. Electrons have a negative charge, and protons have a positive charge. Antimatter is basically just regular matter, but with the opposite properties. So, an antimatter electron (called a positron) has the same size and the same mass as an electron, but it has a positive electrical charge. Similarly, an antiproton has the same size and mass as a normal proton, but it has a negative electrical charge.

Positrons are all around us. Many radioactive elements emit positrons when they decay, and doctors even inject patients with positron-emitting radioactive substances to help diagnose disease. Antiprotons are much rarer. Scientists can make them in a high-energy particle accelerator. Scientists have actually made very, very small amounts of antiatoms by arranging for antiprotons to capture positrons.

As another example, say a lot of electrons are forced through a narrow metal wire. Each electron has a certain amount of energy, and much of that energy will be absorbed by the atoms in the wire. If an atom is heated up, then it contains more energy than it did at a lower temperature. Atoms, like many people, prefer to stay in the lowest energy configuration possible at all times. Some people may stay in a low-energy configuration by sleeping late or by lying on the couch or, if they are asked to exert too much energy, they will lie down. Atoms, on the other hand, get rid of extra energy by giving off radiation. If an atom has extra energy, its electrons will radiate photons, or particles of light. In a traditional light bulb, electricity

What makes antimatter so interesting to scientists and science fiction writers is that it is the most potent fuel known in the universe. This is because when matter and antimatter meet, they destroy each other completely, turning matter into pure energy. This was predicted by Einstein—his famous equation, $E = mc^2$, tells exactly how much energy is released when matter and antimatter annihilate each other. In this equation, E is the energy released, m is the amount of mass that is converted to energy, and c^2 is the velocity of light multiplied by itself (which is what "squared" means). In this case, physicists use special units for c^2, and they say that it is equal to 931 million electron volts (MeV) for every atomic mass unit of matter that is converted to energy. So, a single atom of antihydrogen converted entirely to energy by annihilating a single atom of "regular" hydrogen will release close to 2,000 MeV of energy. These units are not easily understood, so consider this: In the atomic explosion that destroyed Hiroshima, less than one gram of matter was converted into energy. The enormous amount of energy stored in matter is why antimatter is the most potent form of energy in the universe, and it is why science fiction writers chose antimatter to provide the enormous amount of power needed to propel the starship *Enterprise* into warp drive.

heats up tungsten atoms in a metal filament, and its electrons release energy in the form of visible light that comes out of the light bulb. Visible light is radiation because it is a form of energy that travels ("radiates") through space. Visible light is not harmful (unless it is too bright), but it is radiation nevertheless.

Power and Energy

The terms *power* and *energy* are often used interchangeably, but they are two different things. Energy is the ability of a system, such as an electrical plant, to do useful work. Power is the amount of energy the system produces over a given amount of time. So, an electrical plant that delivers 100,000 kilowatts of power produces 100,000 kilowatt-hours of energy every hour. A lightning bolt is very powerful because it delivers a lot of energy over a short time. A nightlight has low power, but it can deliver a lot of energy overnight if it is turned on for hours and hours.

The length of time is very important. One method of measuring energy is the joule. The watt (a unit of power) is equal to using 1 joule of energy in 1 second. So, a 100-watt light bulb uses 100 joules of energy every second. If the same amount of energy—100 joules—is expended in 10 seconds, the power is only 10 watts. On the other hand, if that same 100 joules is expended in 1/10 second, the power is 1,000 watts (1 kilowatt), and if the energy is crammed into a *ten-thousandth* of a second, the power output for that short period of time is a megawatt (a million watts). In each case, the total amount of energy is the same, but the power output varies widely, depending on how quickly the energy is used. For example, exploding a stick of dynamite releases about as much total energy as burning a pound of coal. The reason that a stick of dynamite has so much more power is that all of that energy is released in an instant, instead of over a few hours. Believe it or not, a candy bar contains more energy, pound for pound, than dynamite. However, this energy is released much more slowly as it is digested.

What newscasters (and most people) describe as radiation is actually just one form of the wider world of radiation. Scientists more properly refer to this form as "ionizing radiation." This is radiation (such as X-rays) that has enough energy to "ionize" (remove electrically charged particles from) the atoms it comes in contact with. This ionization can damage genetic material in the body and cause health problems later on in life, such as cancer. Non-ionizing radiation (visible light, infrared, radio waves, microwaves, and so forth) has not been shown conclusively to cause cancer.

Incidentally, it is worth noting that even though there have been some studies that have led people to think that microwaves, radio waves, cell phones, and power lines may cause cancer, all of these studies have eventually been shown to have problems. To date, there are no scientifically convincing studies showing that any of these things actually do cause cancer. This is not to say that it is impossible, just that it seems very unlikely to those who specialize in the health effects of these sorts of radiation. On the other hand, there is no doubt that ionizing radiation can cause health problems.

Classical Ideas of Energy

Energy, as a concept, has been around for a few thousand years. The word itself goes back about 2,500 years to ancient Greece when the scientist Aristotle used the Greek term *en-ergia* to mean "at work." In the early eleventh century, Persian scientist Ibn al-Haytham (also called Alhazen; hailing from modern-day Iraq) published his *Book of Optics*. In it, he proposed that light was a form of energy, though he did not use the term *energy*. Similarly, in the twelfth-century, Muslim scholar Al-Khazini expressed the concept of what we now call "gravitational potential energy," the notion that a rock feels less of Earth's gravity on a mountaintop than on the ground because of its greater distance from Earth's gravitational field.

In the early nineteenth century, the British scientist Thomas Young came up with the modern concept of the energy of motion, or kinetic energy. Young said that an object's kinetic energy depends on its mass and the square of its velocity, a concept that is still taught in classrooms today. Later, with the invention of steam engines, scientists determined how energy efficient they could make these machines. Other scientists showed that energy could take on many different forms. In one of his many demonstrations, the English physicist James Joule dropped a weight in water, which caused a paddle to rotate and showed that the energy of gravity could be converted into the energy of motion.

Figure 4.1 Arab scientist Ibn al-Haytham's most famous work was a seven-volume treatise on optics, called the *Kitab al-Manazir* (*Book of Optics*). In it, he developed a theory that explained the process of vision as rays of light focusing toward the eye from each point on an object.

These ideas, and others, are called "classical." Classical physics has come to mean physics that applies to objects that are larger than atoms and molecules. In the last century, objects the size of atoms and smaller have been described using quantum physics, which is nonclassical.

Classical ideas of energy involve phenomena that would have been familiar to the Ancient Greeks and Romans. These include the concepts of kinetic energy—the energy of motion—and potential energy, which can be thought of as the amount of energy stored in an object. Civilizations identified other forms of classical energy somewhat later. For example, the ancient Greeks knew of static electricity around the sixth century B.C. when the philosopher Thales noticed that objects would become electrically attracted to the hardened tree sap known as amber after it was rubbed with fur (the Greek word for amber is *electron*, which also led to the term electricity). However, Thales and other ancient Greeks had no conception of electrical energy—that electricity could perform useful work such as powering a wheel, for example. By the same token, the earliest humans saw chemical energy being released during combustion, which refers to the burning of fuel. Even the most primitive humans used fire, but people did not understand that fire was the release of chemical energy until just a few centuries ago. In this chapter, we will look at some of these forms of energy to find out what they are and how they work.

One of the most important rules in all of physics is that energy is conserved. This means that energy in the universe is never created or destroyed. The total amount of energy in the universe stays the same, even though it can move from one object to another and change into different forms. (Keeping track of all the energy in the universe is pretty much impossible.) The conservation of energy also applies to any "closed systems," in which energy is not received or sent from the outside environment. So, for example, a ball sitting in a second-floor window has a certain amount of potential energy. When the balls falls from the window, it begins moving faster, picking up kinetic energy. At any point, the amount of kinetic energy the ball gains comes from the amount of potential energy it has lost. The total energy stays the same. When the ball hits the ground, it will bounce, but not quite as high as the window it fell from. Energy has not vanished, but it has changed form. The ball made some noise

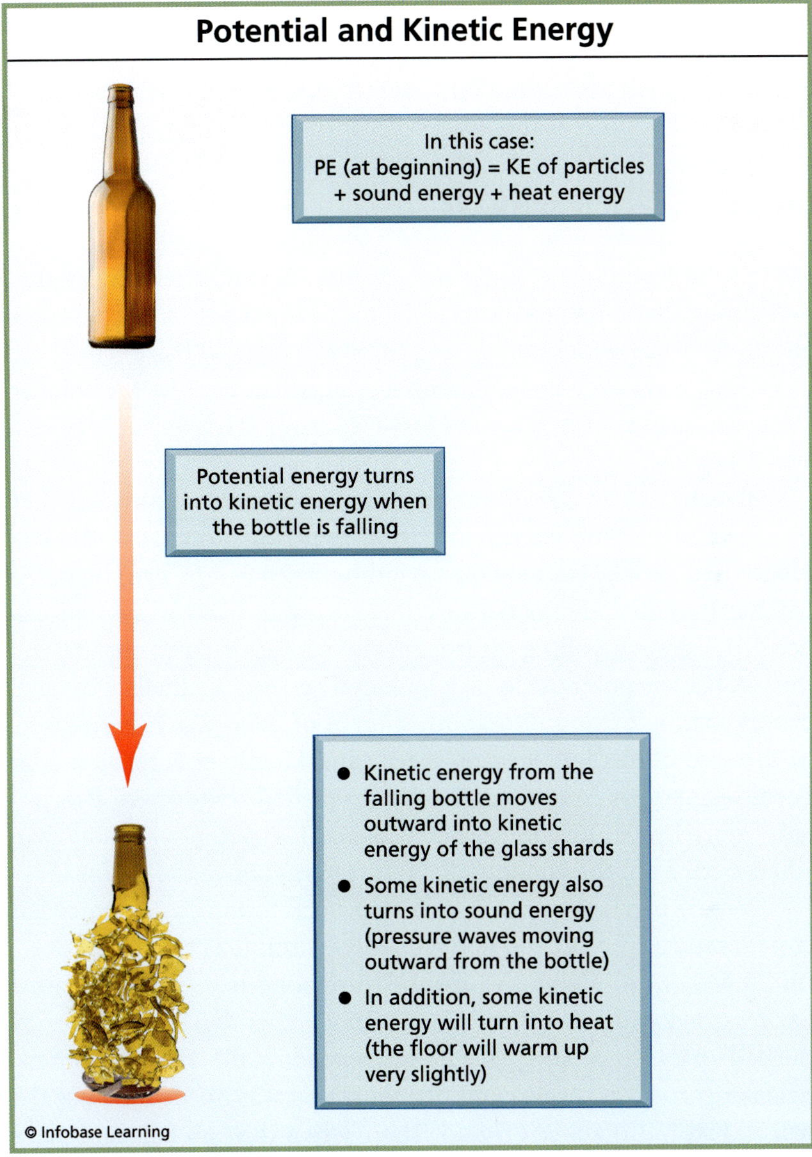

Figure 4.2 Energy forms can either be potential or kinetic. This example shows both at work.

when it hit the ground, and this noise took some of that energy. It may also have compressed the soil a little bit, which takes still more energy. In addition, the ball may also be very slightly warmer, which also takes energy. Adding up the energy lost to noise, compression of the soil, and heat, a careful scientist would find that all of the missing kinetic energy is accounted for. Therefore, energy is conserved.

POTENTIAL ENERGY

Everything begins with potential energy. In fact, one can say that everything that happens in the universe today is a result of potential energy that was generated during the Big Bang and has been stored in various ways ever since. Potential energy can later be turned into many forms of energy, such as kinetic energy or thermal energy (energy from heat).

Objects that are not in motion have no kinetic energy, but they may still have some energy just from their position. Take the ball mentioned earlier: Perched on a windowsill 20 feet (6.1 m) high, the ball has potential energy because it is sitting in Earth's gravitational field. The gravity pulling on it from the center of Earth means that the ball has the potential to pick up kinetic energy as it falls. Potential energy can be turned into another form of energy if it is released. In the case of the ball, it gains speed (and kinetic energy) as it falls. Because energy is conserved, it gets diminished somewhere else. If it falls from a lower altitude, the ball will have less potential energy than when it fell from the windowsill, 20 feet (6 m) above the ground.

Here, it is necessary to take a step back to look at a somewhat larger picture. The ball did not suddenly materialize on the windowsill 20 feet (6 m) above the ground. Someone had to fight against Earth's gravity to put it there. That person expended energy to carry the ball up the stairs and place it on the window sill. Thus, the potential energy really is the amount of energy that was needed to raise the ball 20 feet (6 m) above ground. Then, when the ball falls and picks up speed, this potential energy is turned back into kinetic energy.

Potential energy can also be found in compressed springs. Winding a mechanical stopwatch stores energy in the spring. This energy is stored as potential energy until the button is pushed, at which point the potential energy of the spring is released and becomes the kinetic energy of the moving hand of the stopwatch (plus some acoustic energy if the watch ticks, and maybe some thermal energy if there is friction between the different parts of the watch).

Yet another form of potential energy is chemical potential energy. Eating food, for example, gives us energy. The sugars and proteins in the food give energy to the body, and that energy makes it possible to walk, talk, and do work. One way to look at an apple, for example, is as a package of potential energy waiting to be released. (In fact, the number of calories in the apple is a measure of energy.) In food, this energy is released by metabolism: The body is able to break down chemicals, releasing the energy stored in the chemical bonds. This is also what happens when wood burns—the energy stored in the chemical bonds of a piece of wood is released, turning into thermal energy and the light cast by the fire.

KINETIC ENERGY

Kinetic energy is the energy of motion. *Any* object that is moving—a rolling ball, a falling rock, a car moving down the street, a person on a bicycle, a meteor falling to Earth—has kinetic energy.

What is important about kinetic energy is that it increases very quickly as an object moves more quickly. In mathematical terms, kinetic energy is proportional to the square of the velocity of the object. Squaring a number means that it is multiplied by itself. So, doubling the speed of an object increases its kinetic energy by a factor of 4 (2^2 = 2 x 2 = 4), and tripling its speed increases the kinetic energy by a factor of 9. Thus, in practical terms, this means that a bicyclist riding at 10 miles per hour (16 kilometers per hour) has four times as much kinetic energy as one riding at 5 mph (8 kph), and only one-quarter the kinetic energy as someone zipping along at 20 mph (32 kph). This, in fact, is one reason why it is so much more painful (and dangerous) to run into something at a higher speed. Someone hitting a tree at 20 mph (32 kph), has 16 times as much kinetic energy as someone hitting it at 5 mph (8 kph), which means there is 16 times as much energy to go into causing bruises, cuts, and broken bones (which is why it is important to wear a safety helmet when riding a bicycle, especially at higher speeds!). This is also why catching a fastball can hurt much more than catching a slower one.

Kinetic energy is also proportional to the mass of an object, so doubling an object's mass will double its kinetic energy at the same speed. Thus, a person who weighs 150 pounds (68 kilograms) has twice the kinetic energy as someone who weighs 75 pounds (34 kg) if they are running side by side at the same speed. Putting these two concepts together, it is possible to calculate the kinetic energy of anything: $E_k = \frac{1}{2} mv^2$; or the kinetic energy (E_k) is equal to one-half times the object's mass (m) times the object's velocity (v) squared. Table 4.1 has some examples.

In this table, remember that one kilogram is equal to a little more than two pounds, and that 1 meter per second is equal to about 2.25 miles per hour.

ELECTRICAL, CHEMICAL, AND NUCLEAR ENERGY

The other primary forms of energy are electrical, chemical, and nuclear energy. Of these, electrical energy is probably the most familiar to most people, and nuclear energy is less known. However, chemical energy is probably the most common and the most important.

Electrical energy is what runs televisions, computers, fans, and light bulbs. It powers appliances that are plugged into outlets and

Table 4.1 Kinetic Energy in Various Items			
Object	Mass (kilograms)	Speed (meters per second)	Kinetic energy (joules)
1 quart of milk (0.9 L)	1	1	1
	1	2	4
10-pound (4.5-kg) bag of potatoes	5	1	5
	5	2	20
	5	5	125
Meteor hitting Earth	500	11,200	62,700,200,000 (the same as 15 tons [13.6 metric tons] of explosives)

toys that run on batteries (although in batteries, chemical energy is transformed into electric energy). Electrical energy is carried by electrons moving through space or through any material, usually through metal wires. Each electron has an electric charge, and moving electrical charges create an electric current. Electric current can then provide energy to light a lamp, turn a fan, or run a computer.

Electrical energy is everywhere—not just in electronics and electric motors. Lightning is perhaps the most obvious and spectacular form of natural electrical energy; a lightning bolt carries enough energy to start fires, destroy electronics, and kill people. Electricity flows through the nerves of the human body, making up our

Counterweights and Gravitational Potential Energy

Energy must be expended to carry a ball from the ground floor to the top of a roof. As the ball falls to the ground, it picks up speed (its kinetic energy increases). When it hits the ground, its kinetic energy is equal to the amount of energy that was needed to carry the ball to the rooftop (though, in real-world conditions, it is a little less, as the ball loses some of its energy to such factors as air resistance on its way down).

Even though an elevator may weigh a half ton (0.4 metric ton) or more, it can be moved up and down hundreds of feet by a fairly small motor. The reason this works is that there are counterweights attached to the elevator car, and they are close to the same weight. So, the motor only has to be strong enough to move the difference in weight between the elevator car and the counterweights. Speaking in terms of energy, the gravitational potential energy of the counterweights at the top of the elevator shaft is very nearly equal to the amount of energy needed to raise the elevator to the top. In effect, the falling counterweight provides most of the energy needed to move the elevator. The motor supplies the rest.

thoughts, carrying signals to our muscles, and helping our heart to beat steadily.

Beyond Earth in outer space, charged particles flow outward from the Sun, generating electromagnetic fields as they go. Solar storms (which are flurries of charged particles thrown into space by the Sun) can dump enough energy into Earth's magnetic field to create huge electrical fields that wreak havoc with electrical power grids and electronics. Further out in space, Jupiter's moon Io spews charged particles into space to form a ring around the giant planet. Electric currents also flow through the space around Jupiter. Similar effects have been seen elsewhere in space, in the Milky Way, and even in galaxies hundreds of millions of light-years away. Electrical energy is virtually everywhere in the universe, generated by the movement of electrically charged particles (electrons and protons) through space.

Energy is also present in chemicals, and virtually every substance—water, air, carbon dioxide, and more—is a chemical of some sort or a collection of chemicals. Chemical molecules are collections of atoms that are bound together, and their atomic bonds contain energy. Making new bonds or rearranging existing chemical bonds can release energy. For example, when carbon combines with oxygen, energy is released in the form of heat: This is the process of combustion.

In fact, there can be a tremendous amount of energy stored in chemical bonds. The release of chemical energy drives our cars and airplanes, gives explosives their power, and turns food into energy. Most of the energy used on Earth begins as chemical energy. Even most of our electrical energy begins as the chemical energy found in fossil fuels.

An even more fundamental source of energy is the atomic nucleus. Rearranging the neutrons and protons in the nucleus, splitting a nucleus apart, or fusing two nuclei together releases a tremendous amount of energy, hundreds of thousands or even millions of times as much as breaking chemical bonds. This is why nuclear energy is so powerful: Splitting a single atom releases as much energy as does breaking approximately a million chemical bonds.

One other thing that bears mentioning is that the most general form of energy is heat. Burning produces heat, splitting atoms produces heat, friction produces heat, and electric fields produce heat. When gasoline in a car burns through the process of internal combustion, it produces heat and chemical byproducts. The heated chemical byproducts in the combustion chamber move faster, creating pressure that pushes the engine's piston. The piston moves up and down throughout the engine's cycle, setting the engine in motion and ultimately allowing the car's wheels to move. Thus, the heat of combustion eventually gets transformed into the energy of motion in the wheels of a car.

Einstein's Revolution: Matter is "Frozen" Energy

One of the most famous equations in all of science is Albert Einstein's equation $E = mc^2$. Almost everyone has heard about this famous equation, but fewer people really know what it means, and an even smaller number completely understand it. The short version is that matter and energy are really two different aspects of the same thing—in effect, matter is "frozen" energy, and matter and energy change into each other all the time. Let's look at how this happens.

E = MC² AND WHAT IT MEANS

To start to understand the famous equation $E = mc^2$, the first thing to do is to understand what each of the terms, or letters, stand for. "E" stands for energy, "m" is for mass, and "c" is for the speed of light. The "2" that goes with the letter c means "squared"; that is, the speed of light is squared, or is multiplied by itself. Putting all of this together, this equation tells us how much energy is contained within a bit of matter.

The thought that energy can be contained within matter should not be a strange one. When a log is burned, chemical energy is released to heat up the surroundings. Burning gasoline can drive a car because of the chemical energy stored in the gasoline. In these examples, energy is released by chemical reactions in which electrons rearrange themselves in the atoms and molecules that make up the log and the gasoline. In addition, while these chemical fuel sources take advantage of the energy that is set free when electrons in atoms and molecules rearrange themselves in chemical reactions, nuclear fission and fusion release the far greater amounts of energy that are stored in the very core of the atom—the atomic nucleus. However, there is more going on here, and it directly relates to the $E = mc^2$ equation.

When scientists weigh all of the ashes that are left over from a burnt log, they will find that the ashes weigh less than the original log. However, burning logs also give off smoke and carbon dioxide gas, and these also have weight. Adding up the weights of the ashes, smoke, and carbon dioxide will account for just about all of the weight of the log. Some of the mass of the log gets converted to energy, but in an amount that is almost impossible to detect. However, in nuclear fission and fusion, the conversion from mass to energy is dramatic: The weight of the end product is distinctly less than the weight of the original atoms. Mass is lost when atoms are fused or split apart, and energy is released. This is where Einstein's equation comes in: It turns out that the amount of energy released is related to the amount of mass that is lost. That mass has been turned into energy, and Einstein's equation tells us how much energy is released for each bit of matter.

In Einstein's equation, the key part is the "c^2" because the speed of light is tremendously high (about 186,282 miles per second; or 299,791.2 kilometers per second). If "c" is a large number, squaring makes it much larger; it does not take a lot of mass to give off a lot of energy. Turning a single proton entirely into energy will release about 931 million electron volts (the electron volt is a special unit of energy used in some branches of physics and chemistry). In terms that make more sense to nonphysicists, this equation tells us that converting 1 gram of any type of matter entirely into energy will release more energy than the nuclear explosion that destroyed Hiroshima.

Figure 5.1   In considering a bonfire on a beach, we find that virtually all of the mass of the logs is accounted for after they are done burning by adding everything up (the particles in the smoke, the ashes, and the weight of the gases given off). The heat, sound, and light of the fire come from the chemical energy of the molecular bonds that are broken during the fire and a very small amount of mass that is "missing" because it was converted into energy.

HOW MATTER TURNS INTO ENERGY

Not all conversions of matter into energy are as catastrophic as a nuclear explosion. Fortunately, in fact, there are no everyday, off-the-shelf methods for converting an entire gram of matter into energy, so this is nothing to worry about. Still, we do see matter-to-energy conversion fairly regularly in one of the newest types of medical equipment, a PET scanner.

Despite its name, a PET scanner is not used to scan pets. PET actually means "positron emission tomography." The positrons that this scanner emits are really antimatter electrons. When matter and antimatter meet, they turn into pure energy. The amount of energy released by an electron and a positron is equal to about 1 million electron volts. So, this is one way to turn matter into energy: by making antimatter and letting it come in contact with normal matter.

Another way for matter to turn into energy is to go nuclear. When two protons come together, or fuse, they can form a helium nucleus (a nucleus is the positively charged core of the atom). In this nuclear fusion process, the sum of the whole is less than the sum of the parts. In other words, the helium nucleus is lighter than the sum of the two protons. Where does the missing mass go? It

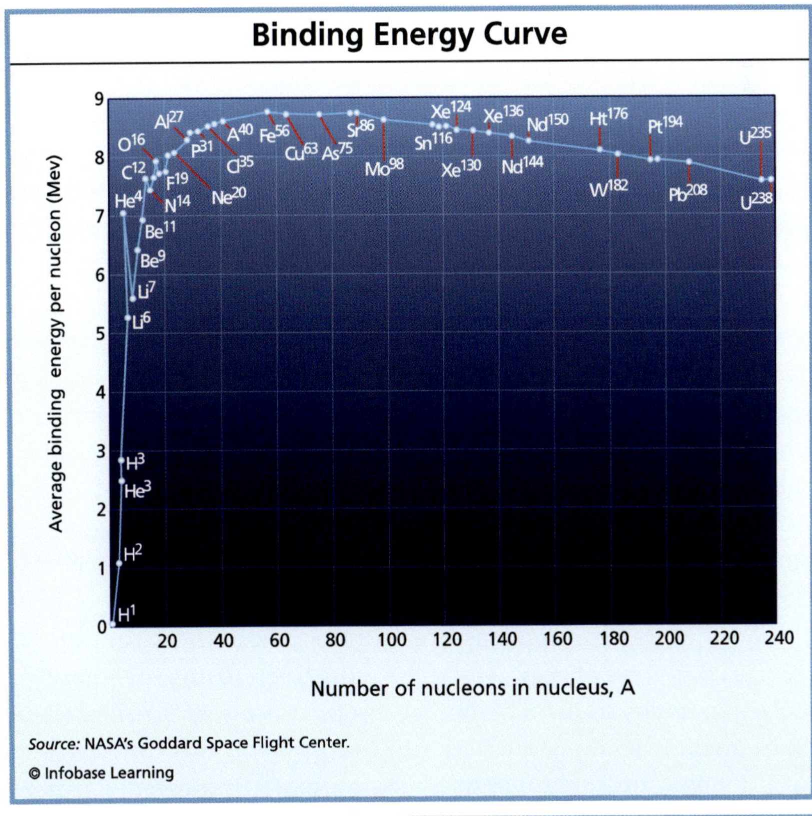

Source: NASA's Goddard Space Flight Center.

© Infobase Learning

Figure 5.2   The binding energy curve is obtained by dividing the total nuclear binding energy by the number of nucleons (neutrons and protons).

	Table 5.1 Mass of a Uranium-238 atom Compared to the Mass of the Parts		
Particle	Number	Mass (each)	Mass (total)
		Atomic mass units	
Proton	92	1.007276466	92.6694
Neutron	146	1.008664915	147.2651
Electron	92	$5.48579909 \times 10^{-4}$	0.0505
		Total	239.9850
		Mass of U-238 atom	238.0508
		Mass difference	1.9342

goes into creating a bond between the two protons that holds the nucleus together. The energy of this bond is called the **binding energy** because it is energy that is released when the parts of the nucleus bind together.

This binding energy is important because it is what makes it possible to get energy from nuclear fusion (the joining together of two nuclei) and the opposite process, nuclear fission (the splitting apart of nuclei, such as those in uranium). This is shown Figure 5.2, which details how the amount of binding energy changes for different elements.

The Binding Energy Curve shows that a single uranium nucleus (atomic number 92) has less binding energy than, say, lighter nuclei of xenon (atomic number 54) and strontium (atomic number 38). So if a uranium nucleus breaks into xenon and strontium, it releases this extra energy. Along the same lines, fusing together two hydrogen nuclei to form helium also releases energy. In all of these cases, mass is being converted into energy—and this difference in mass (shown in Table 5.1) has been measured repeatedly around the world. If we add up the total mass of all of the uranium atoms in an atomic bomb before it explodes and then add up the total mass of all of the atoms formed from nuclear fission, we will find that there is a difference—the fission products will weigh about 0.6 grams less than the original uranium. This 0.6 grams of mass is what was turned into energy. So, going back to the atomic bomb, about one gram of mass was turned into energy in the atomic bomb that destroyed Hiroshima—this energy was emitted in the form of radiation, light, heat, sound, radio waves, and so forth.

HOW ENERGY TURNS INTO MATTER

As already discussed, matter can turn into energy when it meets antimatter, or when the parts of an atom gain energy by joining together. Now, it's time to see how energy can turn into matter, and what that means. In fact, it's actually easier to look at the second question first.

If energy is just another form of mass, then this means that adding energy to an object should make it more massive. So, according to this, anything that adds energy—kinetic energy, potential energy, electrical energy, and so forth—to an object should also make it a little heavier. For example, a charged battery should weigh just a little more than a dead battery, a wound watch (with its potential energy put into winding the spring) should be a little more massive than a stopped (unwound) watch, and so forth. Similarly, heating a 1 kg (2.2 pounds) weight by 1°C (a little less than 2°F) will increase the mass by about 1.5 picograms (there are a million-million picograms in 1 gram, so a picogram is one millionth of a microgram).

Somewhat more esoteric is the fact that Earth's gravitational field also has mass, because the field itself contains energy. In fact, the energy contained in Earth's gravitational field has some mass of its own, and all mass creates gravity. Thus, Earth's gravitational field is a little stronger because of this, compared to the gravity due only to Earth's mass alone. Scientists have actually measured this effect—the mass contained by Earth's gravitational field—in very precise experiments that involve reflecting laser beams from the Moon.

There is another way to convert energy into matter. This method is called **pair production**. When a photon (which has no mass of

(continues on page 56)

Exotic States of Matter: Bose-Einstein Condensates, Superconductors, Superfluids

Virtually everything we come across in our daily lives is made of normal matter, matter that is at a temperature we find comfortable and at a pressure we find survivable. However, under extreme conditions, matter can exhibit properties that seem downright bizarre. The discovery of all of these phenomena astounded scientists and each discovery was considered worthy of a Nobel Prize.

One of the more common of these properties is **superconductivity**. When electric current flows through a wire (or through any other material), it loses energy. As the wire heats up (due to electrical resistance), it takes energy from the electrical current. In fact, electrical resistance can sometimes be useful—it toasts our bread, cooks our food, and lights up homes (in the case of old-fashioned incandescent lightbulbs). However, electrical resistance also robs us of energy; for example, the loss of energy in power transmission lines robs us of about a quarter of the energy produced by the electrical generators. However, at very low temperatures—close to absolute zero—some metals lose all resistance to electrical current; electricity can flow through them with absolutely no resistance. This lack of resistance is called superconductivity. Although some "high-temperature" superconductors have been invented, they must be cooled with liquid nitrogen, which still has a relatively chilly temperature of about −320°F (−160°C). At present, superconductors are most commonly used in MRI units that scan inside the human body. However, if higher-temperature superconductors are ever developed, they may help revolutionize the production and transmission of power.

Another ultra-low temperature phenomenon is called superfluidity. This is where an ultra-cold liquid can flow

Figure 5.3 Researchers have found that superfluid helium, shown in this video screen capture, that has cooled just a few degrees below its boiling point of –452°F (–269°C), is able to do things the average liquid can't. Liquid helium can dribble through molecule-thin cracks, climb up and over the sides of a dish, and remain motionless when its container is spun.

without any resistance at all. For example, this happens to helium when it is cooled to just a whisker above absolute zero, a temperature equivalent to –459.67°F (–273.15°C). Superfluid helium not only flows without resistance, but it can even flow uphill. A container that is filled with superfluid helium will have a thin coating over all its surfaces, including the walls and even the top of the container.

Yet another, even stranger state of matter was theorized in the 1920s by Albert Einstein, but not produced in a

(continues)

(continued)
laboratory until 1995 (the scientists who produced it were awarded the 2001 Nobel Prize). It's called the Bose-Einstein condensate, and it works like this: Every bit of matter also has some wave-like properties; this is how the electron microscope works. The wavelike properties are most easily seen in very light particles, such as photons (which have no mass) and electrons. However, as they become colder and colder, more massive objects begin to exhibit wavelike properties as well. What happens in a Bose-Einstein condensate is that a group of atoms is cooled to the point where their wavelike properties become dominant, and they can coalesce into what is effectively a single "super-atom." The properties of the Bose-Einstein condensate are still being studied, but it is a remarkable new state of matter.

(continued from page 53)
its own) passes close to a heavy atom, it can turn itself into an electron and a positron pair, each of which has mass. Most of the time, the electron and positron almost immediately collide and destroy each other in a burst of energy; this energy is very easy to measure. There is no doubt that pair production—the conversion of energy into mass—takes place because it has also been detected in laboratory experiments.

Physicists take it for granted that mass can turn into energy. They even measure the mass of subatomic particles in units of energy: meaning the amount of energy that is required to form the particles. Using Einstein's equation, an object with a mass of one amu (atomic mass unit) that is turned entirely into energy will release about 931.5 million electron volts (MeV), so a proton (with a mass of 1.007276466 amu) will release 938.27 MeV if it is turned into energy. Thus, in the parlance of particle physicists, a proton has a "mass" of 938.27 MeV. The mass and equivalent energy of some subatomic particles are shown in Table 5.2.

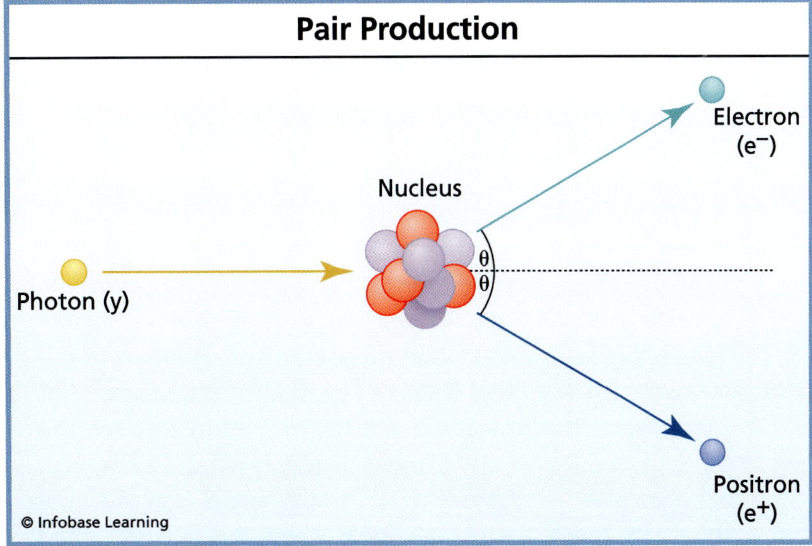

Figure 5.4   In physics, pair production is a phenomenon in which energy is converted to mass.

Table 5.2 Mass of Selected Subatomic Particles (and Their Equivalent Energies)

Particle	Mass (atomic mass units)	Energy (MeV)
"up" quark	0.00322	3
Electron neutrino	2.147×10^{-8}	<0.000002
Electron	0.0005486	0.511
Proton	1.0073	938.27
Neutron	1.0087	939.57
Muon	0.1135	105.7
W particle	86.3124	80,400
Z particle	96.8331	90,200

Strange Happenings: Pair Production, Virtual Particles

One way to convert energy into matter is through the formation of electron-positron pairs. This formation occurs when a high-energy photon passes close to an atomic nucleus. Even stranger things can happen: For instance, particles can pop out of nowhere and then vanish again. While this seems to violate the law of conservation of energy (which says that energy can neither be created nor destroyed), the process is actually permitted through the laws of physics. What happens is that, in effect, a small bit of energy is "borrowed" from empty space (the vacuum) to create these "virtual particles"; then, this debt is repaid when the particles vanish back into the nothingness from which they came.

Strange as this process seems, the presence of virtual particles can be detected. Under some circumstances, pairs of virtual particles can be made "real" if they are pulled apart before they can annihilate each other (as in the case of an electron-positron pair). In addition, virtual photons can appear very close to a radio antenna and affect the electrical current that is generating the antenna's radio field. Virtual particles are also responsible for something called the Casimir effect, where scientists can actually measure a very slight force that is exerted by virtual photons on very closely spaced, thin, metal plates. All of these are evidence that virtual particles, while unexpected, really do play a role in our universe.

While converting energy into matter is not as (literally) explosive as converting matter to energy, it also has been observed and measured by scientists.

Particle Explosion

A particle accelerator in Europe called the Large Hadron Collider (LHC) is one of the largest and most complicated machines ever built. Like previous accelerators, it will be capable of accelerating subatomic particles to just short of the speed of light and smashing them together, but at unprecedented speeds and energies. When particles collide in an accelerator, they form still more particles. A lot of attention is paid to these particles because they form the foundation for everything that exists in the universe—not only objects that can be seen, but those that cannot be seen. What these particles are and how they interact with one another not only control what matter is and how it behaves, but may actually hold clues to the fate of the universe.

THE PARTS OF THE ATOM

What is the smallest thing in the universe? According to Democritus and his teacher Leucippus, who were philosophers in ancient Greece around the fifth century B.C., the smallest things in the universe were "atoms." In the ancient Greek language, *atom* means "indivisible" (meaning it can't be broken down into smaller parts). Democritus and Leucippus thought that a variety of tiny, invisible atoms made up everything that is seen in nature. Philosophers in ancient

India, at around the same time, had a similar concept. A classic book from that time, the *Bhagavad Gita*, states that the material world was made of 24 different elements.

Centuries later, these notions remain remarkably close to the truth. Atoms are the main building blocks of our material world, and there are many varieties—more than 100 of them, in fact. Modern scientists, however, realize that atoms, as we know them today, are made of smaller parts. Echoing ancient concepts, however, some of these parts cannot be further divided in any known way.

All atoms are made of smaller particles: Protons and neutrons are located in the nucleus, and electrons are on the atom's outskirts. The number of protons determines the identity of the atom. An atom that contains one proton is a hydrogen atom. An atom with 6 protons is a carbon atom. The number of protons is also called the **atomic number**.

Protons have a positive electrical charge, electrons have a negative charge, and neutrons have zero charge. Atoms are electrically neutral: In an atom, the number of electrons is equal to the number of protons; the positive and negative charges cancel each other out.

Electrons are arranged around the nucleus of an atom in a particular way; they follow very specific rules as far as how far from the nucleus they orbit and how many electrons are permitted to be at each distance. As an example, think about a house that is filling up with guests. Maybe eight people can fit into the kitchen, but only two are allowed in each bedroom, and only one at a time can occupy the bathroom. So, as guests arrive, they are sent to various rooms, with instructions to fill up each room in turn, starting with the smaller rooms, with maybe one to each closet, two to a bedroom, six in the kitchen, and so forth.

Electrons do the same thing as they fill the orbitals, which are the locations around the nucleus that the electrons can orbit. The first two electrons fill the innermost orbital, the one closest to the nucleus. The next four go to the next level, and so forth. This is important because the chemical properties of an atom are determined by the way the electrons are arranged around the nucleus. Atoms are most stable—the state in which they are least likely to form chemical bonds—when their outermost orbital is completely filled. This is the configuration of the "noble" gases like helium and argon, which typically do not combine to form molecules with other atoms. At the other extreme, atoms are most chemically reactive when the outermost orbital has only 1 electron, or when it needs only 1 electron to be filled. This is what chlorine and potassium—two of the most chemically reactive of the elements—have: a single electron or a single electron missing in their outermost orbitals.

The number of protons determines the identity of the atom. The number of electrons in an atom controls an atom's chemical properties. So what do the neutrons do?

All protons have a positive electrical charge, and because they have the same charge, they repel each other. Anyone who has played with magnets knows that the north pole of one magnet will attach to the south pole of another magnet, but it will be repelled by another north pole. This works with electrical charges, as well; two positive charges repel each other. It should not be possible to stick two protons together because the closer they get to each other, the more strongly they push each other apart. This means that it should be impossible to have atoms with more than a single proton. There must be something else going on—some sort of force that helps hold the atoms together. This force is the strong nuclear force. The strong nuclear force is stronger than the electrical force, but it only works over a very short distance—inside the nucleus, which is much smaller than the size of an atom. Thus, for the strong force to do its job, the protons have to be very close together in the nucleus.

The strong nuclear force is part of the makeup of protons. They not only try to force themselves apart with the electrical force, but if they get close enough, the strong nuclear force helps hold them together. However, the strong force carried by protons is not enough to overcome the electrical force and hold the nucleus together. More strong force is needed than the protons can carry, and every time another proton is added to the nucleus, the amount of electrical force is also increased. Therefore, any atom larger than hydrogen (which has just one proton in its nucleus) would simply fly apart if the nucleus contained only protons.

This is where the neutrons come in. Neutrons have no electrical charge, so adding them to the mix increases the amount of strong force without having any impact at all on the electrical force. In other words, the neutrons in an atom help to make possible the existence of larger atoms such as iron, gold, mercury, and lead. An

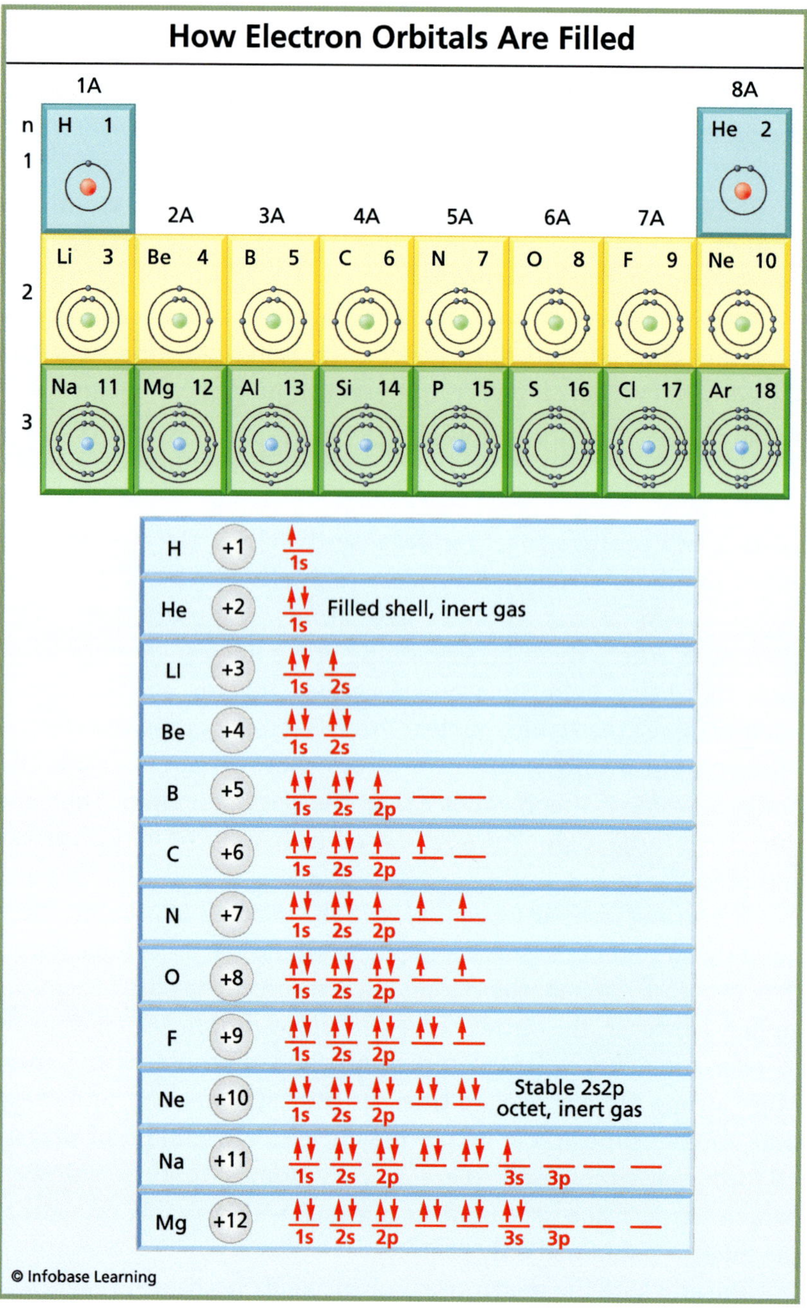

Figure 6.1 These figures show two different ways in which electron orbitals can be filled.

atom with too few (or too many) neutrons won't hold together for long—it will release particles and become smaller and simpler in order to reach stability.

NEUTRINOS

You have already read about the concept called conservation of energy, one of the most important concepts in all of science. Physicists are convinced that the total amount of energy in the universe (including the energy contained within the mass of all of the universe's objects) never changes. Energy can change its form (dropping a ball, for example, changes potential energy into kinetic energy), and energy can form matter, but the total amount of energy in the universe never seems to change.

In each type of atom, neutrons, protons, and electrons all occupy very specific energy levels, and the laws of physics do not let them occupy levels in between. Someone on a staircase, for example, can stand on step 3 or step 4, but it is not possible to stand halfway between two steps. Furthermore, the distance between steps 3 and 4 is precisely defined. It is easy to calculate exactly how much potential energy a person on step 3 has, how much potential energy they have on step 4, and to calculate how much energy they gain (or lose) by moving from one step to the other. Therefore, scientists measuring the potential energy of a person going up a step would see that it increases in discrete amounts; they would not expect to see a half-step's worth of energy. In just this way, energy given off by atoms appears in discrete chunks—called quanta—that are exactly equal to the difference in energy between one state and another.

Given all of this, imagine the surprise of scientists who, while measuring the energy of a type of radiation called beta radiation, realized that beta particles don't follow this rule. Beta particles are really just high-energy electrons or positrons (the antimatter version of electrons) released from radioactive atoms. Scientists found that the radioactive atoms released beta particles with a smooth, continuous range of energies. Thus, the beta radiation released from, for example, phosphorus-32 (a radioactive form of phosphorus) might have energy equal to a million electron volts (MeV), energy of a half MeV, 1.5 MeV, and so forth. In fact, they could have any energy at all, up to a point—the maximum energy that beta radiation from this sort of atom could have is about 1.7 MeV. Interestingly, the difference in energy between the phosphorus-32 "parent" atom and what it decays to is 1.7 MeV—the beta particle that is ejected from the atom takes with it the extra energy held by the radioactive phosphorus atom.

Scientists could understand seeing a beta particle with this maximum energy—it was precisely what they expected to see *every* time. What they could not understand was how they could possibly see any *other* energy. After many experiments, the scientists were confident that they were not making mistakes in their experiments, and they had not yet seen evidence of any other radiation given off. This left them with two possibilities, neither of which they liked. One possibility was that, along with the beta particle, the atoms were also emitting another ghostly particle that was invisible to even the best instruments. The other possibility was that energy disappeared when beta radiation was emitted from the atom. Although scientists were not happy to think about particles that could not be detected, the idea that energy might not be conserved was even more unsettling. Ultimately, the scientists decided that energy must be conserved, and they named the mystery particle the **neutrino**. Although neutrinos were first hypothesized in 1930, it was not until 1956 that science and technology advanced to the point of finally being able to detect them.

Today, physicists know that there are three different types of neutrinos: the electron neutrino, the muon neutrino, and the tau neutrino. For many years, physicists thought that neutrinos might have no mass at all—like photons—and that they would travel at the speed of light. However, experiments in the 1980s and 1990s have shown that neutrinos travel slower than light, and that they have a very small amount of mass. The electron neutrino is the most common form of neutrino. It is given off during beta decay and has a mass that is only a very tiny fraction of the mass of the electron (which is, itself, about one-two thousandth the mass of a proton or neutron). The heaviest neutrino, the tau neutrino, is more massive than an electron, but is still far lighter than almost any other particles. Table 6.1 summarizes the properties of the fundamental particles that make up what physicists call the **Standard Model** of particle physics; the sidebar describes a little about how these particles are related to one another.

Table 6.1 Fundamentals Particles			
Family	Particle	Mass (MeV)	Comments
Quarks	Up	2.4	Elementary particles: combinations of three quarks make up protons and neutrons. Quarks carry electric charge and are responsible for the electric charge of protons.
	Down	4.8	
	Charm	1270	
	Strange	104	
	Top	171,200	
	Bottom	4200	
Leptons	Electrons	0.511	Leptons are paired so that (for example) electrons and electron neutrinos occur together. In some forms of radioactive decay, both the electron (beta particle) and electron neutrino are emitted from the nucleus of an unstable atom. Heavier pairs (muon and tau) are seen only in high-energy environments and not in normal matter.
	Electrons neutrino	0.000002	
	Muon	105.7	
	Muon neutrino	0.17	
	Tau	1777	
	Tau neutrino	15	
Bosons	Photon	0	Carries electromagnetic force
	Gluon	0	Carries strong nuclear force that helps hold atomic nuclei together
	Z	91,200	Carries weak nuclear force that helps hold together the quarks that make up protons and neutrons
	W	80,400	

Note: Physicists measure the mass of subatomic particles in units of energy (millions of electron volts, or MeV). This is the amount of energy that is produced if each of these particles is converted entirely to energy using Einstein's equation, $E=mc^2$. One thousand MeV is equal to 1 GeV (giga-electron volt).

The "Particle Zoo": Three Families of Matter

To date, scientists have found an enormous number of particles; the ones mentioned in this chapter are only a few. However, all of the particles that have been identified are either "fundamental" particles (particles that cannot be broken down any further, such as quarks and electrons), or they are particles that are made of various combinations of fundamental particles. It may be helpful to think of them in terms of a Lego set: Although there are only a few basic types of Lego pieces, they can be combined to build an amazing variety of structures. In the same way, the relatively few types of particles that exist can be combined to form all of the other particles, all of the atoms, and all of the matter that we see in the universe.

Four fundamental particles "carry" forces. The photon, for example, transmits the electromagnetic force, the gluon carries the strong nuclear force, and the W and Z particles carry the weak nuclear force (which is responsible for some forms of radioactive decay). These force-carrying particles are also called bosons. Six more fundamental particles are supplied by the different types of quarks, which combine to make objects such as protons and neutrons. Electrons, muons, and tau particles are three additional fundamental particles, and they each have their own different type of neutrino that often form with them during radioactive decay. Together they provide another six particles that are called leptons. All in all, the Standard Model of particle physics (Figure 6.2) contains 16 known types of particles from among the three "families" of particles: 6 leptons, 6 quarks, and 4 bosons. If the Higgs boson is discovered, there will be 17 confirmed types of fundamental particles.

There may yet be more particles to be discovered. In fact, all particles have antiparticles (anti-electrons, anti-protons, anti-muons, etc.). Some scientists have proposed that *all* of these particles—matter and antimatter included—have "superpartners," which would roughly double the

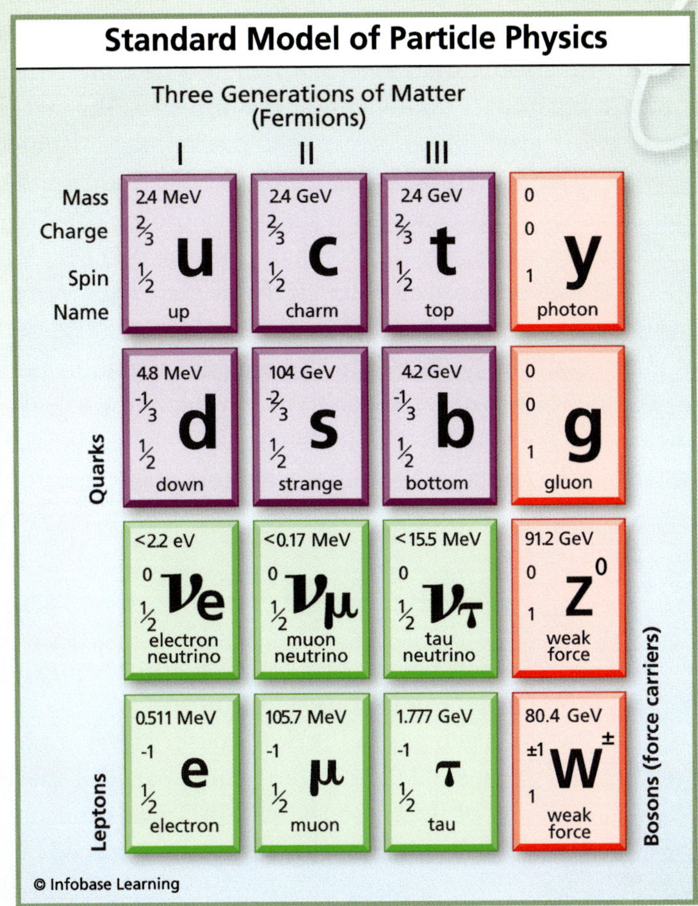

Figure 6.2   The Standard Model of particle physics offers a framework for analyzing the universe in terms of matter (fermions) and force (bosons).

number of known particles. For example, the photon would have a companion called the "photino," the gluon would have the "gluino," and so on. These "superpartners" have remained hypothetical so far, but with the construction of the world's biggest collider—Europe's LHC—scientists will be able to search for these particles and find out if they really exist. Watch the news and view science publications to see if these or any other new particles are discovered!

What is interesting is that, although neutrinos are the least massive of all particles, they are also the most numerous particles in the universe. This means that, even with such a tiny mass, neutrinos may have a big impact on the fate of the universe. The fact that the universe exists at all places some boundaries on how much mass a neutrino can have. In the parlance of physics (remembering that matter can change into energy), a stationary proton has a "mass" of 938 MeV, and a stationary electron has a mass of 0.511 MeV (1 MeV is equal to 1 million electron volts). If the average energy of the neutrinos is any more than about 50 electron volts (0.000005 MeV), the total mass of all the neutrinos in the universe would be enough to cause the universe to collapse due to the strength of the gravity of all the neutrinos. Amazingly, a sizeable chunk of the total mass in the universe may be contained within the lightest of all particles.

COSMIC RAYS AND MUONS

Our Sun is a huge, hot ball of gas, and it is always spraying mass into space. This "solar wind" consists of mostly protons and electrons from the hydrogen gas in the Sun's outer layers. Traveling at up to 500 miles per second (804.7 kpm), these particles reach Earth in a few days. Many of them are trapped by Earth's magnetic field to form the Van Allen radiation belts; many are absorbed by Earth's atmosphere, sometimes causing the Northern Lights; and some of them reach the ground. The Sun is only one source of cosmic radiation, the radiation that comes from outer space.

Not much of the Sun's cosmic radiation reaches sea level because very few of the particles have enough energy to penetrate through the entire atmosphere. Surprisingly, most cosmic radiation is accelerated by the remnants of exploding stars (supernovae) that are found elsewhere in our galaxy. When a star explodes, it creates long-lasting clouds of gas and magnetic fields. Particles encountering these magnetic fields can accelerate across the galaxy, slam into our atmosphere, and still reach sea level. (However, most of the time, the cosmic ray hits atoms in the atmosphere and breaks up; nevertheless, its energy is transmitted to the ground, just as the energy of a pool ball may go into breaking up the racked balls, which then transmit that energy to the other end of the pool table.) Most of the cosmic radiation measured at sea level originated across the galaxy, and not in our own solar system. Even though, on Earth, most of the cosmic radiation fails to reach the ground, in space it can be deadly. Plans for long-duration space missions must include the protection of astronauts from the effects of the solar storms they may very well encounter.

When cosmic rays slam into the atmosphere, the result can be very much like what happens in a particle accelerator. Scientists have detected the results of these collisions, and one of the particles they frequently find is not normally seen outside of powerful accelerators: This particle is called the muon. Muons are much like electrons, but they are 200 times more massive. In fact, muons are far too massive to be produced naturally on Earth. They are produced by either high-energy particle accelerators or through cosmic ray collisions in the atmosphere. Much of the cosmic radiation measured at Earth's surface comes from these muons. In fact, they can even penetrate *into* Earth and have been detected up to nearly 0.6 miles (1 k) deep in solid rock.

This finding actually surprised many scientists because muons have a very short lifetime once they are created; in fact, the average muon lasts for only a few microseconds (millionths of a second). By the rules of classical physics, if they could travel at the speed of light, they would only live long enough to travel 1,500 feet (457 m) or so. In fact, the detection of muons at sea level helped scientists prove one of the more remarkable claims of Einstein's **special theory of relativity**: Time slows down for objects moving close to the speed of light. Cosmic ray muons, it turns out, travel so quickly that time slows for them. Instead of decaying far above the surface of Earth, they last long enough for them to travel more than 60 miles (95.6 k) to Earth's surface, and up to a half mile (0.8 k) deeper into the ground.

This ability to go straight through matter has led some scientists to propose using muons for scanning cargo containers for the presence of illegal nuclear or radiological weapons. While these experiments are still ongoing, it is possible that, before too much longer, muon detectors will help to make us safer. This is truly a remarkable thought—that a particle blasted from an exploding star halfway across our galaxy, that can survive a millennia-long passage through tens of thousands of light-years of space, can slam into a molecule

Figure 6.3 This bubble-chamber photograph shows particle tracks from a cosmic ray collision. Cosmic radiation occurs when Earth is bombarded by particles from the Sun as well as particles from exploding stars (supernovae) elsewhere in the galaxy.

in the atmosphere above our heads to create a muon—and then that very muon might be sent zipping through a shipping container to reveal the presence of a terrorist's nuclear weapon.

QUARKS AND GLUONS

Finally, in this somewhat abbreviated tour of what is sometimes called the "particle zoo," we come to **quarks** and **gluons**. Remember neutrons and protons, the particles that make up the nucleus of the atom? They are, in turn, made of quarks. Quarks appear to be one of the fundamental building blocks of all matter. In other words, they can't be broken up into smaller parts.

The terminology that applies to quarks is somewhat confusing, and it can even seem silly. There are six kinds of quarks: "top," "bottom," "up," "down," "strange," and "charm." (The top and bottom quarks are sometimes also called "truth" and "beauty.") These different kinds of quarks are referred to by their individual "flavors"; so, a charm quark is said to have a different "flavor" from a top quark.

Quarks don't exist alone, but they group together in threes (forming objects called baryons, which include neutrons and protons) and also in pairs (called mesons). Recent experiments provide evidence that quarks sometimes join together in groups of four called "tetraquarks."

Quarks also have an electrical charge, and this is what gives protons their electrical charge and neutrons their lack of a charge. Inside a proton there are three quarks. Two of these quarks are up quarks and the third is a down quark. Adding up the electrical charge (+2/3 for an up quark, -1/3 for a down quark) gives the +1 charge on a proton. Neutrons, which still have a quark of each flavor, contain one up and two down quarks, with the charges adding up to zero ($+2/3 - 1/3 - 1/3 = 0$). This is why neutrons have no electrical charge.

Therefore, the proton and neutron are actually not fundamental particles; rather, they are made up of even smaller parts. (However, electrons, the other major component of the atom, are believed to be indivisible.) If the proton and neutron are made of smaller parts, then what keeps them together?

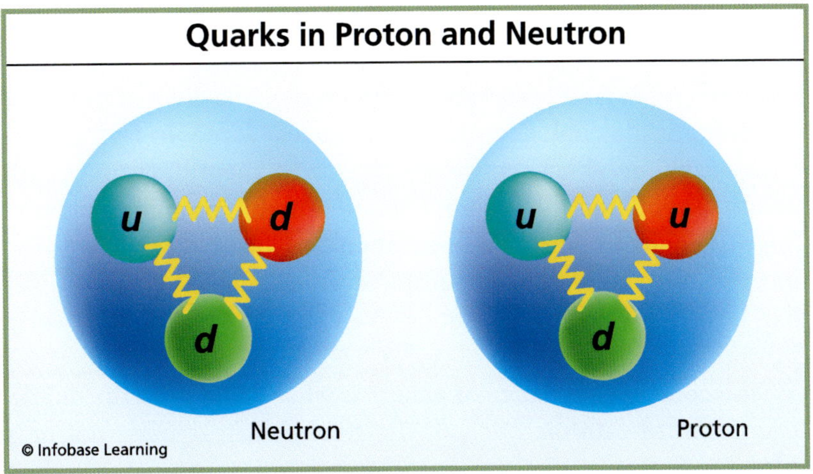

Figure 6.4   This illustration shows the quark structure of a neutron (*left*) and a proton (*right*). "U" stands for an "up" quark, while "d" represents a "down" quark.

Figure 6.5 American physicist Murray Gell-Mann received the 1969 Nobel Prize in physics for his work with elementary particles.

In addition to supplying an electrical charge inside neutrons and protons, quarks provide an equally important function: They help exert the strong nuclear force that holds together nucleons—the protons and neutrons that make up the nucleus—by emitting particles called "gluons." Quarks are always exchanging gluons, and these gluons are responsible for the strong nuclear force. In fact, quarks exchange gluons almost continuously—up to a septillion times each second (a septillion is a trillion trillion, or a million billion billion). This makes gluons one of the most abundant kinds of particles in the universe, and they exist right inside every atom. The physicist Nathan Isgur was referring to gluons when he said, "Most of the world is made of glue."

The constant exchange of gluons is what helps keep the quarks together in the atomic nucleus; the strong nuclear force not only helps hold groups of nucleons (protons and neutrons) together, but more importantly, it helps hold the groups of quarks together, even though protons and neutrons both contain two quarks with the same electrical charge. Most importantly, the strong force helps hold together the protons and neutrons; what holds the nucleus together is the remaining force that leaks out of the individual neutrons and protons.

The strong force is so strong that it actually keeps quarks confined within particles. This is called quark confinement, because the quarks are, in effect, prisoners confined within the neutron and proton and are unable to escape on their own.

Our understanding of quarks has evolved with time. They were first proposed and named by Nobel Prize-winning physicist Murray Gell-Mann in 1964 as a way to explain some of the properties of particle physics, although at that time, only three flavors of quarks were proposed (up, down, and strange). Later, in 1970, Sheldon Glashow (another Nobel laureate) and others suggested that there might be another quark. This one turned out to be what is now called the charm quark. The last addition to the family of quarks came in 1973, when the top and bottom quarks were proposed. They helped explain some otherwise mysterious phenomena seen in particle accelerator experiments. Although most physicists accepted the reality of quarks, it took time to prove it; it was not until 1995 that physicists at Fermilab saw evidence of the most elusive quark of all, the top quark.

Matter and Energy in the Universe

The universe is made of matter and energy; energy can be turned into matter and matter can be turned into energy. Cosmologists—scientists who study the origin, evolution, and ultimate fate of the universe—are deeply interested in the history and future of matter and energy in the universe. What they are beginning to understand boggles the mind.

Right after the Big Bang, the universe was much smaller than today. Matter was packed so densely that energy was trapped in it. When a particle released energy, such as a particle of light (a photon), the light would be absorbed by a nearby particle and couldn't travel very far. About 380,000 years after the Big Bang, as the universe expanded and cooled, charged particles joined together and formed neutral atoms of hydrogen and helium. Photons were no longer immediately absorbed by matter. They could now bounce off the atoms and escape into space. Amazingly, we can still see this light from the early days of the universe. It's called the cosmic microwave background radiation. You can see some of it in a fraction of the "snow" that appears on a television set that is hooked up to an old-fashioned antenna (not cable TV).

Approximately 400 million years after the Big Bang, the first stars formed, and the nuclear fusion in their cores produced heavier elements, all the way to iron. When these stars ran out of fuel and died,

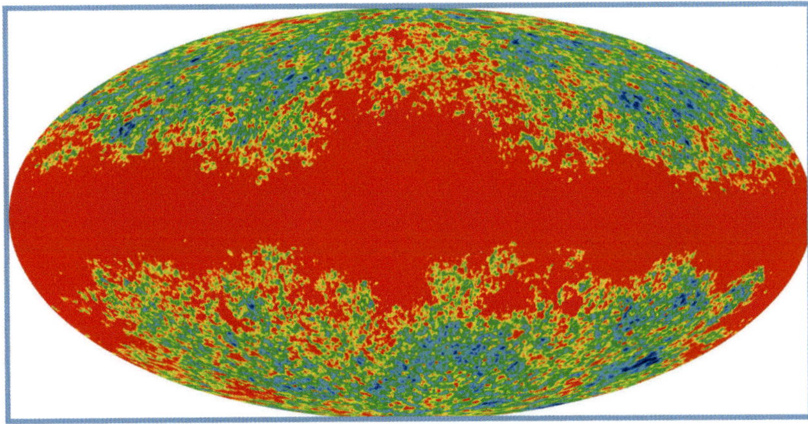

Figure 7.1 This full-sky K-band map shows the cosmic microwave background radiation and foreground contamination from our galaxy (in red).

the most massive of them exploded into supernovae. In these titanic explosions, heavy elements such as lead, uranium, plutonium, and even heavier ones, were formed and sprayed into space. All of the atoms that form Earth (or, at least, everything heavier than helium and a little carbon) was formed inside of stars and expelled with the dying star's last gasp. The death of stars can also form even stranger forms of matter, such as neutron stars, **black holes**, and possibly even stars composed entirely of quarks.

MATTER AND ITS EFFECTS ON THE UNIVERSE

Matter dents the fabric of space, like a steel ball resting on a rubber sheet, and the larger the mass, the bigger the dent. For example, Earth dents the space around it. Lighter matter, such as a nearby meteor, effectively rolls "downhill" into the dent; we see this as a gravitational attraction from Earth. Space is almost infinitely flexible—a tremendously large mass will create a dent or warp in space that extends millions or billions of light-years. Our galaxy is being pulled

Figure 7.2 This composite image uses data from three of NASA's observatories. The Chandra X-ray image is shown in light blue, the Hubble Space Telescope optical images are in green and dark blue, and the Spitzer Space Telescope's infrared image is in red. The neutron star is the bright white dot in the center of the image.

by an immense mass called the Great Attractor. This mass is located more than 200 million light-years away. In other words, it would take light, which travels at 186,000 miles (299,338 km) per second, more than 200 million years to reach the mass.

Isaac Newton was the first to imagine that every bit of matter exerted a pull on every other bit of matter in the universe. In the story of Newton and the apple tree, Newton's great insight was to realize that, as Earth was pulling on the apple, the apple was simultaneously pulling on Earth. However, because Earth is so much more massive than the apple, the apple falls toward the ground, while the ground only moves imperceptibly toward the apple. By the same logic, Earth pulls on the Moon, which, in turn, pulls on Earth.

In fact, the results of the Moon's gravity can be observed: Earth and the Moon both orbit around a common point, but because Earth is so much more massive than the Moon, that point is actually located inside of Earth.

In our solar system, every planet pulls gravitationally on every other planet. However, the pull of the Sun, the most massive object in our solar system, controls the path of every planet, all of the asteroids and minor planets, comets, and even interplanetary dust and gas. The path of the Moon around Earth is controlled by Earth's gravity (just as the other planets control the orbits of their own moons in our solar system), but the Sun also exerts a pull on the Moon. More importantly, even though the Moon orbits Earth, the path of Earth is controlled by the pull of the Sun. This means that the Moon's large-scale motion is controlled by the Sun's influence on Earth.

That being said, remember that every planet pulls on every other planet. The Sun may be the most important gravitational body in the solar system, but Earth also feels the pull of Jupiter and, to a lesser extent, the pull of every other planet. However, even though every planet pulls on every other planet, their mass is so much less than the Sun's, and the result is that their pull is mostly limited to their nearest neighbors.

From a point right outside the solar system, the gravitational force mainly comes from the center—the Sun—the location of most of the mass in the solar system. The Sun's gravitational influence reaches out about two light-years, to the point where the gravity of the next nearest star, Alpha Centauri, begins to take over. Since the Sun and Alpha Centauri are both about the same mass, their gravity is about equally strong at a point halfway between them. Still further out, the Sun and other nearby stars pull on other, farther stars. Zooming out to the entire Milky Way galaxy, we can see that the visible galaxy is enveloped by a large cloud of invisible "dark" matter that contains much of the Milky Way's gravity. (There will be more on this in Chapter 8.) And, on an even larger scale, the matter in and around our galaxy pulls on the matter of the other 30 or so galaxies in our local group of galaxies, which, in turn, is part of a supercluster of galaxies that are pulled by the Great Attractor mentioned earlier.

Every bit of matter in the universe exerts a gravitational pull. Even though the gravity of a planet, or even a star, may be small, the cumulative effect of this pull is immense. The gravity of the Milky Way galaxy is the sum total of the gravity of every part of our galaxy, both the visible as well as the invisible parts. And our galaxy, in turn, adds to the sum total of the gravity of the universe.

Over time, the fate of the universe will be decided in part by the *total* amount of matter it contains, as well as the mysterious phenomenon called dark energy (discussed in Chapter 8). The universe began expanding outward with the Big Bang, but whether it eventually collapses again depends on the total amount of gravity generated by all of its matter and energy. If there is enough matter and energy, the universe will eventually collapse again; if not, it will continue to expand forever. The current evidence suggests that the universe will expand forever, thanks in part to the dark energy that seems to be forcing the universe to expand ever faster over time.

Thus, the ultimate effect of matter on the universe is to warp space, create gravity, and help regulate the rate at which the universe expands. Planets, stars, galaxies, and even clusters of galaxies all dance to the music of gravity, and gravity is determined primarily by the presence of mass.

ENERGY AND ITS EFFECTS ON MATTER

Earlier in this book we talked about how matter can become energy, and how energy can turn into matter under the right circumstances. Still, there is more to the story than that—energy can have an effect on matter, even without one changing into the other.

Energy can be absorbed by matter. One example of this is when a microwave oven gives off microwaves, a form of electromagnetic energy. These microwaves are absorbed by water molecules in the popcorn (or coffee or dinner) in the oven. As a result, these water molecules gain energy and transfer it to neighboring atoms and molecules, causing them to move faster. As the atoms and molecules move faster than surrounding matter, they become hotter. The temperature of matter is really a measure of the kinetic energy of its molecules. (The molecules of hot objects have more kinetic energy than those of cold objects.) Therefore, the faster the atoms and molecules move, the warmer that object becomes. So, in a microwave oven, the energy contained in the microwaves is absorbed by the water molecules in the food, causing them to vibrate, which is what causes the food to warm up.

In fact, the most common effect that energy has on matter is to heat it up. Energy can come from photons—particles of light—such as the photons that travel all the way from the Sun to Earth to heat up a beach on a summer day. This process of transferring energy from a hot object (the Sun) to another object (the beach) over a distance (that is, without direct contact) is called radiation.

Heat energy can also be created by friction. Actually, friction is much more familiar to most people than photons are. (For example, think of how campers make a fire by rubbing two sticks together.) With friction, energy (usually kinetic energy) is transmitted directly from one object to another. Some other examples of how friction works can be found in how your hands warm up when you rub them together. A car's tires heat up from their friction against the road, and a meteor burns up in the atmosphere due to its friction against the air (which is why the Space Shuttle needs to be covered with protective tiles). In all of these cases, kinetic energy is being transformed into heat energy through a process called **conduction**. The name comes from the fact that the energy is conducted directly from one object to another, instead of from a distance.

There is yet another way to transfer energy (and heat), and it typically occurs in a fluid, such as air or water. As a fluid warms, it rises because it has become less dense (which is why hot-air balloons rise into the sky). As the warm fluid rises, cool fluid is drawn in from the sides. Then, when the warmer fluid reaches the cooler fluid, it transfers its heat energy to the cooler object. This process is called **convection**. This is the third way that energy can be transferred

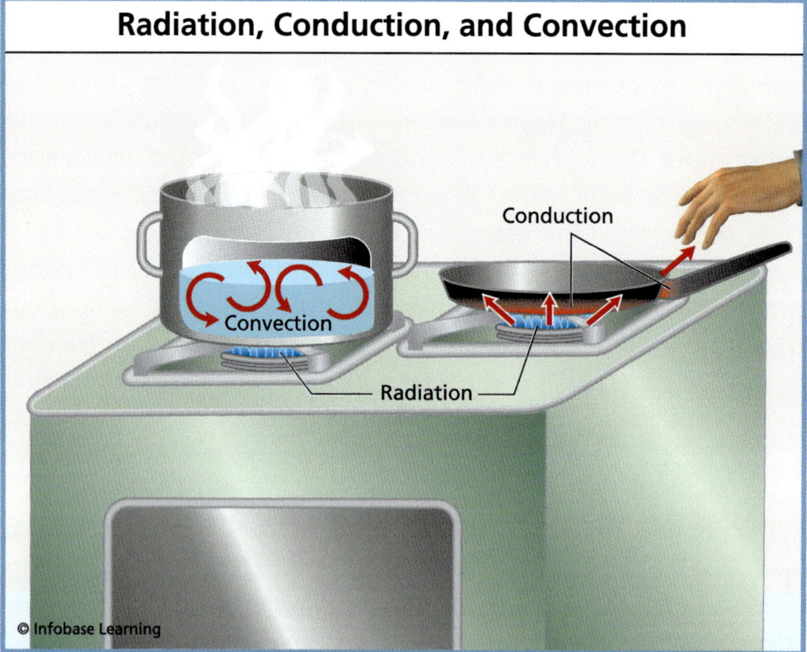

Figure 7.3 Energy (heat) is transferred between Earth's surface and the atmosphere by radiation, conduction, and convection—all of which are shown in this illustration.

from one object to another in the form of heat. One way convection can be seen is in an electric space heater, which transfers its warmth to the cooler air in a room.

Let's think about how energy interacts with matter to make life possible. The Sun transfers energy to Earth by radiation, keeping our planet warm enough to support life. This same transfer of energy helps plants to undergo photosynthesis and keeps them (and all the animals that eat them) alive. When the daytime (and summertime) air warms up, it rises and spreads out, which not only creates winds and the rest of our weather, but also helps to keep the night side of Earth habitable; in contrast, the Moon's night side (which has no atmosphere) is usually much too cold (more than -350°F, or -212°C) and its day side is far too hot (higher than 250°F, or 121.1°C) to support life. Without the convection taking place in Earth's atmosphere, temperatures on our planet would be just as uncomfortable. In fact, much slower convection is also responsible for the shape of the continents, as well as for most volcanoes and many earthquakes. In this case, the core of Earth conducts heat to the lower levels of the mantle, which undergoes very, very slow convection. When the mantle material nears the surface, it spreads out and pulls the continents with it, forming oceans. At the far side of the oceans, the mantle has cooled and begins to sink down again. (It is in these locations that the deepest points in the oceans are found.) As the mantle sinks down and heats up, it melts to form magma, which then rises back to the surface to erupt from volcanoes. All of this activity is driven by very slow convection, and it takes tens of millions of years to complete a single cycle.

These are examples of how energy interacts with matter on Earth, in contrast to the universe-controlling aspects of matter that were mentioned earlier. However, these same processes—conduction, convection, and radiation—happen all over the universe. Hot, young stars give off large amounts of radiation, which heats up nearby clouds of gas and dust to hundreds of thousands or millions of degrees. When matter spirals in toward a black hole or a neutron star, it is not only heated by radiation, but it can also be heated by friction with other gases contained in the accretion disk. In many cases, this gas can be heated to millions of degrees. We can even see convection taking place in stars. Most stars produce energy and heat only in their innermost layers, and the heat from the star's core drives convection in its outer layers, just as heat from Earth's core drives the convection of the mantle. Astronomers see examples of convection and radiation everywhere they look in the universe on scales ranging from planets to entire galaxies. Conduction, the most familiar form of energy transfer on Earth, may actually be the rarest form of energy transfer in the universe as a whole. We see conduction on Earth because there is so much matter and it is easy for atoms to bump into one another. In the vacuum of space atoms are so far apart that they don't bump into one another very often—in space (which is most of the universe) energy is mostly transferred by radiation.

ENERGY'S EFFECTS IN THE UNIVERSE

For hundreds of years, scientists have known that mass helps to hold together the universe and determine its shape and behavior. The Sun's gravity holds together the planets in the solar system—and the Sun exerts enormous gravity because of its very large mass.

However, according to Einstein's principles, energy is equivalent to mass. Remember that, in pair production, a high-energy photon can turn into an electron and a positron. This tells us that this amount of energy (about 1.022 million electron volts) is equal to a very small mass, in this case, about 1.82×10^{-31} kilograms.

Why We Have Matter in the Universe Today

In the very early universe, there was only energy. As the universe expanded and cooled down, it became possible for matter to form. However, during pair production, photons form both electrons and positrons—matter and antimatter—in equal amounts; matter and antimatter go on to destroy each other. Most physicists believe that the formation of any form of matter should result in the production of matter and antimatter in equal amounts. This is referred to as symmetry. To provide an example, a rectangle is symmetrical because it looks the same when it is turned upside down or flipped over. In physics equations that describe the conversion of energy into matter, there is a symmetry that says that particles and antiparticles should be produced in equal amounts. This is what the mathematics says should happen, but we know that the math must be wrong.

The reason that we know the math is wrong is because we exist! If matter and antimatter were *always* formed in exactly equal amounts, then every bit of matter would

Now think about what this means. A charged battery has more energy than a dead battery, so a charged battery should have just a little more mass than a dead battery. The amount of energy in a battery is fairly small, so, in practical terms, it is not possible to measure the increased mass in a charged battery because there is just not enough of a difference when compared to the mass of the battery itself.

However, at cosmic scales, energy can have a profound effect. According to some recent astronomical observations and theories of how the universe is constructed, nearly three-fourths of the total

(continues on page 86)

have its own bit of antimatter. This means that they would destroy each other, and the universe would be filled with nothing except energy. Since we exist, and because we can see matter all around us, we know without a doubt that, for some reason, there was just a little more matter formed than antimatter; in fact, it seems that for every 1,000,000,000 atoms of antimatter that were formed, there were 1,000,000,001 atoms of matter. This is an incredibly small margin, but it is responsible for everything we can see (and much of what we can't see) in the universe.

The existence of matter makes physicists believe that at least one particular symmetry must not exist in a pure form—that, in the earliest moments of the universe, the symmetry must have broken, resulting in unequal amounts of matter and antimatter. This discovery, which has been tested in the laboratory, won the Nobel Prize for its discoverers. Unfortunately, it can account for only a tiny fraction of the matter that can be seen in the universe. It seems that scientists still do not understand this aspect of physics as well as they would like, but they can determine how much nature's symmetries are broken. Important experiments in this area are continuing.

Black Holes

Many museums, zoos, and similar institutions display exhibits of bright yellow funnels down which visitors can drop a coin and watch it roll into an ever-tightening spiral until the coin finally falls through the hole in the center. Once the coin is dropped, there is no turning back—it will spiral down until it finally vanishes into the collection box. Now, replace the coin with a ray of light and the funnel with the strongest gravity known to exist in the universe and you have a black hole. Nothing can escape from a black hole—not even light.

Black holes were first thought of in 1783 by the English Reverend John Michell, and, independently, by the French physicist Pierre-Simon Laplace. Both realized that it might be possible to have a gravitational field so strong that it would even capture light, although neither could think of exactly how this might happen.

A black hole forms when a massive star (several times as massive as our Sun) runs out of fuel and collapses. In many cases, the outer layers of the star will blow out into space in a supernova explosion, and the remainder is forced into an ever-smaller volume. As the star gets smaller and smaller, the gravity increases tremendously: Assuming that the mass of the star remains the same, the gravity increases by the inverse square of the star's size. When the star shrinks to half its original size, gravity is four times as strong; at one-tenth the size, gravity is 100 times as strong. It is easy to see how this process can run away, with the gravity growing so quickly that the star never stops shrinking. Essentially, the star shrinks to what is called a *singularity*—a point in space with (theoretically) a volume of zero and a gravity that is almost infinite. What happens then is anyone's guess. Some scientists think that black holes effectively dig themselves a hole through space and crawl inside.

Every black hole has a point of no return. Matter spirals in (usually forming a disk of hot gas—the accretion

Figure 7.4   This optical and infrared image from the Digitized Sky Survey shows the crowded field around the micro-quasar GRS 1915+105 located near our galaxy. The inset shows a close-up of the Chandra image of GRS 1915+105, one of the brightest X-ray sources in the Milky Way galaxy. This micro-quasar contains a black hole about 14 times the mass of the Sun that is feeding off material from a nearby companion star.

disk mentioned earlier) just as a coin spirals down the yellow funnel. As the matter gets closer, the gravity increases and the escape velocity increases. Eventually, the gravity is so strong and the escape velocity is so high that not even light can travel fast enough to escape. This point is

(continues)

(continued)

called the event horizon: Nothing that crosses the event horizon (not even light) can ever escape into the "normal" universe again.

Astronomers have found that black holes are common in the universe. Virtually every galaxy seems to have a huge (called super-massive) black hole at the center, and they can be millions to billions of times as massive as our Sun. In addition, there are garden-variety black holes that are anywhere from several times as massive as our Sun up to tens of times as massive. "Stellar-mass" black holes have been found around several stars in the Milky Way, including stars designated as Cygnus X-1 and SS-433.

(continued from page 83)

amount of mass and energy in the universe may consist of mysterious dark energy. As the next chapter will show, the shape and the ultimate fate of the entire universe may be controlled by an exotic form of pure energy.

New Matter and Energy

Everything that can be seen in the universe, everything that scientists have spent centuries learning about, may only be comparable to the froth on a huge cup of hot cocoa. This is because what makes up almost all of the universe cannot be seen and can barely be detected. In the last few decades, scientists have come to understand that there is much more to the universe than the "typical" forms of matter and energy that have been known for a hundred years or more. Even more importantly, the ultimate fate of our universe probably depends on unseen and exotic forms of matter and energy. Imagine spending your entire life in a home, coming to know every nook and cranny, every hiding spot, and every detail of your home. Then, one day, you wake up and find out that what you thought of as "home" was only a very small apartment in a huge skyscraper. At the moment, this is where we find ourselves, and we are trying to find the "key" to start exploring the rest of the building.

This chapter will describe efforts to learn more about these new forms of matter and energy—and, more importantly, how they might affect the universe.

THE DISCOVERY OF DARK MATTER

The laws of planetary motion date back four centuries—all the way back to the days of Johannes Kepler, Galileo Galilei, and (most importantly) Isaac Newton. Their work seemed to explain the motions of planets and moons in the solar system as well as the motions of stars across the universe. One of the fundamental parts of these laws is that the speed of any orbiting object depends on its distance from, and the mass of, the object it is orbiting. So, in our solar system, Mercury orbits the Sun more quickly than Earth does because Mercury is closer to the Sun than Earth is. Furthermore, according to Newton, if the Sun were even more massive, all of the planets (in their current orbits) would orbit at faster speeds.

Extending these laws further into space, astronomers found that they could be applied to other stars. For example, when two stars orbit each other, their speed also seems to depend only on the distance between these "binary" stars and their masses. (In fact, this is one way to "weigh" a star; scientists can calculate the mass of a star by measuring the distance to a companion star and its orbital velocity.) Thus, when astronomers first began to try to calculate the mass of entire galaxies, it was natural for them to first measure the velocities of stars at a variety of distances from the galaxies' centers.

Remember: The speed of an orbiting object depends on its distance from the center of the mass it is orbiting and on the amount of that mass. In our solar system, most of the mass is concentrated in the Sun, right at the center. In a galaxy, the mass is spread out, and the orbit of every star is affected by the mass "inside" its orbit (that is, between that star and the center of the galaxy), as well as by the mass "outside" its orbit. So, calculating the expected speeds of stars in a galaxy is somewhat more complicated than calculating the orbiting speeds of the planets in the solar system, but it can be done. Astronomers first expected to find that stars located at greater distances from the center of the galaxy would move more slowly than those located near the center, similar to what happens in our solar system. What astronomers actually saw was astonishing—after a certain point, the stars' velocities stopped dropping and just leveled off. After carefully checking their calculations and their measurements, the only explanation that made any sense at all was that each galaxy was embedded in the midst of a huge cloud

Figure 8.1   This composite image shows the galaxy cluster 1E 0657-56, also known as the "bullet cluster." The dark matter is blue, while the normal matter is pink. The blue is actually where the dark matter is calculated to be based on studies of this part of space.

of invisible matter—matter that could not be seen, but that exerted a gravitational pull. This was analogous to the thinking that led to theorizing about, and later discovering, the neutrino. Faced with two choices, one impossible and the other implausible, scientists chose to believe the implausible because there simply was no other option. Once again, scientists found themselves believing that there had to be something invisible and nearly impossible to detect, and that it was very important to our understanding of the universe. Since the matter could not be seen, it was given the name *dark matter*. From there, scientists quickly determined that the universe contained about ten times as much dark matter as it did the stuff that our sun, our planet, and all of us are made of.

Once astronomers accepted that dark matter made up most of the matter in the universe, they and physicists began to wonder about its exact nature—what could possibly be so widespread, yet invisible? They quickly began to accumulate a list of suspects, ranging from the ordinary to the exotic.

When looking at galaxies, scientists can most easily detect stars, and whatever objects they happen to light up (such as nebulae; not everything in the universe is equally visible). In a distant galaxy, for example, astronomers can see only the very brightest stars; dim stars, planets, and the clouds of gas and dust between the stars are pretty much invisible. In fact, there are many objects that scientists can't even see in our own galaxy, let alone in galaxies that are millions to billions of light-years away. In addition to the objects contained within the galaxies, there is a lot of gas in between the galaxies as well. However, if a certain type of matter can't be seen, how can scientists measure it? It turns out that some of this matter can be detected indirectly. For example, the light from distant galaxies passes through "empty" space on its way to Earth. However, if that space happens to be filled with gas and dust, some of the galaxy's light will be absorbed, and other light will be reddened. Something similar occurs at sunset, when the sun's light, passing through more gas and dust in Earth's atmosphere, becomes redder and dimmer. Thus, when astronomers look at a distant galaxy and measure the light very carefully, they can see evidence of this reddening and dimming. This is one way to start to estimate the amount of matter in the tremendous voids between galaxies. When astronomers first started measuring all of this light, they were able to account for some of the "missing mass"—but not nearly all of it. Thus, they continued looking.

Other objects, such as planets and dim stars, are present as well, both in solar systems and between stars. Astronomers began looking for them in the Milky Way galaxy and decided that they also contributed a portion of the missing mass—but again, not enough to account for all of the dark matter they calculated must be present to account for the speed of rotation of galaxies. The search for dark matter continued.

Planets, gas, dust, and dim stars are all made of "normal" matter: in other words, matter that radiates some form of light. With the sources of normal matter accounted for, scientists began thinking about what else might be out there. One possibility was that dark matter was made of exotic particles that simply can't be directly detected. Neutrinos were one of the possibilities. In fact, there are so many neutrinos in the universe that, even if each neutrino has a mass that is just a whisker more than zero, they could account for some of the missing mass in the universe. Even when counting neutrinos, though, there is still a lot of matter that is simply unknown. Physicists have suggested the existence of all sorts of exotic dark-matter particles, but because they have not yet been detected, they remain guesses. One possible class of dark matter is called Weakly Interacting Massive Particles—WIMPs for short. WIMPs would be very hard to detect because they would pass through normal matter as though they were ghosts going through walls—still, they would exert enough gravity to help keep galaxies together. Strange as it seems, we might actually live in a WIMPy universe!

By proposing dark matter, scientists thought that they had accounted for most of what was in the universe—but they were wrong.

DARK ENERGY

By the 1990s, astronomers were accumulating an impressive array of new tools. Among them were larger ground-based telescopes, many of them equipped with "adaptive optics," which helped to compensate for atmospheric turbulence that could distort starlight. There were also orbital observatories such as the Hubble Space Telescope. With these increasingly sophisticated tools, astronomers were finally able to start trying to answer more and more difficult questions. One of these was to try to find out if the expansion of the universe was slowing down and, if so, how quickly this slowdown was happening. This was another way to try to measure the amount of dark matter in the universe. If the universe began with a single Big Bang, everything in it was given an incredible "push" at the beginning of time. Cosmologists wanted to find out if the universe would keep expanding forever, or if there was enough matter to create enough gravity to someday pull the universe back together in a "Big Crunch" at the end of time. To understand how scientists decided to answer these questions, though, it is first necessary to discuss how stars explode, and how the universe is expanding—in other words, to learn a little about supernovae and the **Hubble Constant**. However, it might make more sense to start with the second concept first.

In the 1920s, American astronomer Edwin Hubble began measuring the brightness of a certain kind of star, called a Cepheid variable. This type of star was so bright that it could be seen even in other galaxies. They were predictable in that it was possible to calculate exactly how bright they were by making precise measurements as the stars cycled from brighter to dimmer. Measuring the apparent brightness of a Cepheid enabled Hubble to calculate its distance: Cepheids that looked somewhat dim were more distant; ones that looked brighter were closer to Earth.

At the same time, astronomers were realizing that they could learn about the chemical composition of stars by studying the light they gave off. Each element gives off light with a specific "color": Hydrogen, for example, gives off red light (among other colors), while oxygen emits green light (among others colors). In fact, every element has a number of very specific colors of light that it emits, and this pattern of colors is like a fingerprint—each pattern is distinct. By carefully studying the range of light (called the spectrum) coming from the distant stars, astronomers could determine which elements were present.

At some point, astronomers began to see that the spectra of stars in distant galaxies were not what they expected. They saw, for example, something that looked like the "fingerprint" of oxygen, but all of the lines were shifted toward red. They finally realized that they were still seeing oxygen, but that the light had been stretched out by the Doppler shift so that what began as green light was shifted into yellow or orange. After more work, they realized that this "redshift" meant that distant galaxies were moving away from us. And, when Hubble added his work on galactic distances to the work on galactic redshifts, he realized he had made a shocking discovery: The entire universe was expanding, and the further away a galaxy was from us, the faster it was moving.

Hubble also noticed that the speed of the galaxy's retreat increased in a steady manner, so that a galaxy twice as far away was moving twice as quickly. With enough observation, Hubble and later astronomers realized that this rate of speed could be predicted: The Hubble Constant gave astronomers a way to calculate how quickly the universe was expanding. Not only that, but it also gave astronomers a way to help determine when the universe was born, and even, possibly, the universe's ultimate fate. A large Hubble Constant

Figure 8.2   American astronomer Henrietta Swan Leavitt was the first to understand how to calculate the actual brightness of Cepheid variables.

would show that the universe was expanding very rapidly, suggesting that it was young and had not yet had a chance to slow down too much after the original Big Bang. A small Hubble Constant, on the other hand, would tell astronomers that the universe was older and had expanded at a slower rate. Yet whether the universe expanded quickly or slowly, they all expected that this expansion was losing steam and gradually slowing down.

So astronomers set themselves to the goal of pinning down the value of the Hubble Constant. The way to calculate this value was to learn how quickly galaxies other than our own are moving away from us. This would tell us how quickly the universe is expanding—and how the expansion rate has changed over time—and it's where modern astronomers come into play.

In the late 1980s, scientists came up with the idea of using supernovae—exploding stars—to measure the expansion rate of the universe. Some types of supernovae, called Type Ia, seem to always explode in the same manner and seem to always have exactly the same brightness. (In fact, a single supernova can shine as brightly as an entire galaxy.) Like Cepheid variables, the brightness of a supernova can be used to determine the distance to a distant galaxy: the dimmer the supernova, the more distant the galaxy. These scientists used the brightness of supernovae to determine the distance to a galaxy, and used the Doppler shift of light from the galaxy to calculate how quickly it is moving away from us. These could be plotted on a graph to learn how quickly the universe is expanding; from this, they hoped to learn how old the universe was and the value of the Hubble Constant.

What the scientists found surprised not only them but virtually every other astronomer in the world. They found that the most distant (oldest) galaxies were moving the most rapidly and the ones at medium distances were slowing down, exactly as expected. Then came the surprise—at some point in the universe's history, the rate of expansion seemed to speed up again. Closer (and younger) galaxies were moving away from us faster than expected. In other words, the expansion of the universe was slowing down up to a point, exactly as expected—and then it began to speed up again. What makes this amazing is that, according to theory, there was only so much energy released in the Big Bang, just as there is only so much energy put into rolling a ball up a hill. Just as a ball slows down and then starts to roll back down, so too was the universe expected to be slowing down steadily with time. To find a ball suddenly starting to speed up as it rolled uphill would be, to say the least, a surprise. Yet they found the universe was doing just that—after a point, it was starting to "roll uphill." Repeated observations proved this to be the case; the question was, how and why?

After years of research, astronomers and physicists finally concluded that the only possible answer was that there was something else at work in the universe; they found that the universe was not only full of matter and dark matter, but something else that physicists called dark energy. Dark energy is odd, indeed. While it permeates the entire universe, it is, so far, undetectable to even the most advanced instruments. In addition, it is somehow helping to power the ever-faster expansion of the universe.

According to some recent experiments and theories of how the universe is constructed, nearly three-fourths of the total amount of its mass and energy may consist of this dark energy. Many scientists have proposed that dark energy gives the universe the extra outward "push" that flattens it.

The more that scientists studied dark energy, the stranger it turned out to be. Why, for example, did the universe slow down at first and then speed up again? Why was this energy so different from other forms of energy? Why can't astronomers detect it? And what are its properties?

At the moment, the answer to most of these questions is "we don't know." That said, there are some things about dark energy that *are* known. One fact is that while normal matter and dark matter clump together into stars, planets, and galaxies, dark energy seems to be spread evenly through the entire universe. It also seems that dark energy is immune to most of the forces that affect regular matter; it doesn't emit or respond to electrical or magnetic forces, and it doesn't seem to emit or respond to the strong and weak nuclear forces, either. In fact, except for its effect on the speed of the universe's expansion, dark energy seems to remain remarkably aloof from everything else.

The other property that scientists can figure out about dark energy is that it is incredibly rarified; dark energy has an equivalent energy concentration of about 4.2 protons for every cubic meter. This is emptier by far than the best vacuum that can be made on Earth, and it is only because the universe is so large that dark energy can exert such a huge influence.

Keep in mind that scientists have not yet directly observed dark energy. Yet, to many of them, it is the best explanation for both the universe's expansion rate and its flatness.

Scientists are still scrambling to try to understand what dark energy is and how it works. At the moment, the best guess seems to be that dark energy is simply the energy that is wrapped up in space itself—that space has some inherent amount of energy. However, nobody is really sure, and this is one of the great things about science: Nearly three-quarters of our universe is made up of stuff that can't be seen, can't be detected, and that science only just became aware of. Just think: Someday, a scientist will finally understand what dark energy is; that person will help the rest of humankind understand what makes up the majority of today's universe.

DARK ENERGY AND THE INCREDIBLE EXPANDING UNIVERSE

Remember that Edwin Hubble discovered that the entire universe is expanding. This, along with other evidence, convinced astronomers that the universe began with a Big Bang that set in motion the very expansion that Hubble discovered. For decades, the biggest questions in cosmology (the branch of astronomy that looks at how the universe began, how it will end, and what will happen in between) had one major question: How would the universe end? In response, astronomers could think of only a few options. They felt that the universe would expand forever, just stop (or keep slowing and eventually stop), or collapse back on itself in a "big crunch." Cosmologists realized that each of these scenarios could tell them something about the shape of the universe. A universe that would expand forever was called "open" and its shape could be imagined as an infinite saddle, spreading outward in all directions; a universe that would someday collapse was called "closed" and its shape would be like a huge ball; and a universe that would someday stop expanding but not collapse back was called "flat" and resembled a sheet of paper. Some astronomers secretly hoped that the universe would be closed—leading, presumably, to another Big Bang and the ultimate in cosmic recycling.

In the past few decades, some very sophisticated satellites have been launched to help map the shape of the universe. These satellites have found that the universe is largely "flat." In a flat universe, two photons that travel in parallel lines from one end of the universe to another stay parallel (as long as their paths are not bent by local pockets of space curved by gravity). However, there does not appear to be enough mass and energy in the universe to make it flat. Without enough mass and energy, the universe should be "open." In this scenario, two parallel photons would slowly spread out even if gravity does not bend their paths.

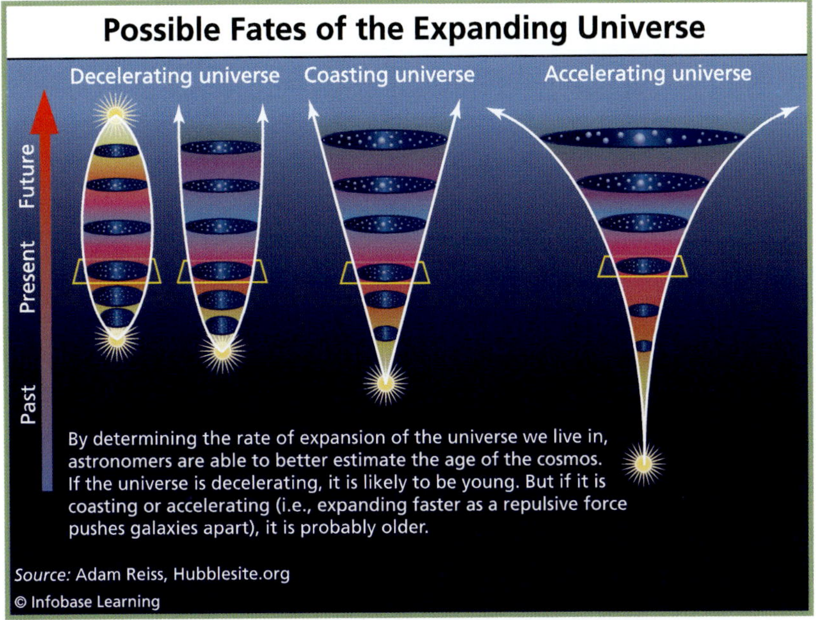

Figure 8.3 By determining whether the universe is slowing down (*left*), coasting along (*middle*), or speeding up (*right*) its expansion, and combining this knowledge with other observations of the cosmos, scientists can better figure out the universes's age.

However, in a "flat" universe, space would continue to expand until it finally slowed to a stop at some unimaginable time in the future. Think, again, of rolling a ball up a hill: In a closed universe, the ball would run out of steam and roll back down to the bottom; in an open universe, the ball would keep rolling uphill (although more and more slowly all the time); and in a flat universe, the ball would come to a stop at the top of the hill. However, when the evidence was in, it seemed that the correct answer was "none of the above."

Imagine, if you will, throwing a ball into the air, watching it rise up, slow, and then fall back down. Now, what if the ball rose, slowed down, and then speeded up again? Most people would be surprised, to say the least! Still, this is exactly what the universe seems to be doing. At first, the expansion of the universe behaved exactly as expected. The supernova project showed this conclusively. The surprise was that, after a few billion years of slowing down, the expansion began to accelerate.

Dark energy could explain both things—it provides the outward "push" to cause the expansion of the universe to accelerate, and it also provides the extra energy needed to flatten its shape. It would take a lot of dark energy to accomplish both of these processes. Current estimates suggest that the universe's dark energy outnumbers all other forms of matter and energy by about three to one!

It took astronomers a while to accept this because it ran so against what anyone expected to find. Nevertheless, one of the hallmarks of science is that good scientists will accept the evidence they are shown. This acceptance may take awhile, but most scientists will eventually change their minds when it becomes obvious that they are wrong. The same principle holds true with the debate about dark energy and the ever-expanding universe. After several years of trying to refute the evidence and trying to find alternate explanations, scientists had to accept that the universe was speeding up as it got older. In this line of reasoning, dark energy hardly existed in the early universe, but it now makes up almost three-quarters of all matter and energy. Accepting this idea, scientists are still trying to understand exactly what dark energy is and what properties it has. They are also back to some of the same old questions, including "What will be the ultimate fate of the universe?" Except that now, the possible answers are a bit odder than the ones they first learned about.

THE ULTIMATE FATE OF THE UNIVERSE

At the moment, the universe is expanding faster and faster with time. Thus, it is natural to wonder if this acceleration will continue and, if so, if this expansion will keep speeding up. This scenario is sometimes called the "big rip," and some scientists think that as the universe keeps speeding up, first the more-distant galaxies will drop out of view, then the closer galaxies, and then our nearest neighbors will vanish over the horizon. As time goes on, and the universe speeds up even further, even our own galaxy will be torn apart, and maybe even the solar system, planets, and atoms themselves. The thing is that nobody knows. Astronomers simply don't know enough about how dark energy works to have any idea what sort of

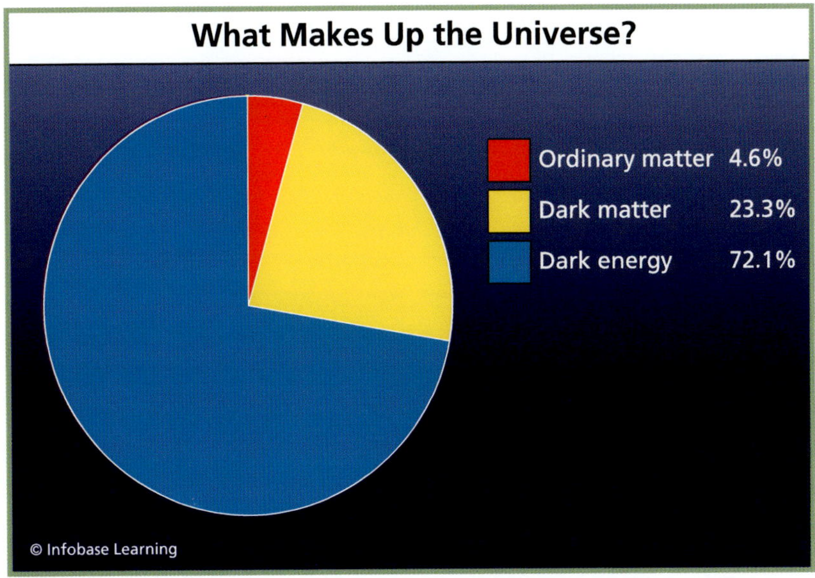

Figure 8.4   Only about 4.6% of the universe's mass comes from the ordinary matter that makes up planets, stars, and gases.

role it will have as the universe continues to age and expand. Unless there is something very odd and unexpected yet to be found, it seems likely that the universe will continue to expand forever, making the universe either "open" or "flat." However, there is no telling when another astounding discovery will make us reconsider even this assumption. Whatever happens, the expansion of the universe seems to be fueled by the most mysterious thing astronomers have yet discovered—dark energy.

Why Is There New Matter?

Energy and matter are the two fundamental ingredients in the universe. Energy can travel by itself over billions of light-years in space, or it can reside in objects for billions of years. Energy exists in all matter, from the atoms and molecules that make up apples to the far tinier cores of atoms, as well as in chemical bonds. (These bonds can be thought of as "frozen" energy.) And, strangest of all, the secret to the ultimate fate of the universe itself might be found in nothingness—in the energy that pervades empty space.

Matter can be as familiar as a soccer ball or as small as the tiny particles that make up everything. It can be as huge as the galaxies and the vast clouds of dark matter in which they reside. And, just as most of the universe appears to be made of mysterious dark energy, so is most of the matter made up of something that we can neither see nor detect. The Standard Model of particle physics seems to explain just about every type of matter that has been detected, but it does not explain dark matter. As successful as it has been, the Standard Model leaves many important questions unanswered. Thus, let's close the discussion with a look at some of the mind-boggling new things that go beyond the Standard Model—concepts such as supersymmetric particles, string theory, and the extra dimensions that these would require to explain their existence—and take note of what the world's most powerful particle accelerator might discover.

SUPERSYMMETRIC PARTICLES

Quantum mechanics (which describes the world at the scale of atoms) and the **general theory of relativity** (which describes the nature of gravity at the scale of the universe) are two of the most spectacularly successful theories in science. Time after time, scientists have tested these theories and their scientific predictions, and time after time, these predictions have been found to be correct—even when they seemingly defy common sense. General relativity, for example, predicts that light can be bent by gravity, a fact that was confirmed in 1919 during a solar eclipse. Quantum mechanics predicts that a single photon passing through an experimental apparatus will act differently if its path through the apparatus can be traced, and that matter at times can act like waves. These predictions have been confirmed over and over again in laboratories around the world. Together, these two theories seem to explain all four of the fundamental forces in nature and the behavior of virtually everything in the universe. However, to a scientist, almost is not quite good enough. Science demands a single theory that explains everything, as opposed to two theories that explain *almost* everything. And, in spite of their success, these theories have some glaring problems that just call for new physics.

One of the problems with the current understanding of physics is that quantum mechanics deals with just three of the fundamental forces of nature (electromagnetism, the strong nuclear force, and the weak nuclear force), but not gravity. In general relativity, gravity is defined as the way that matter warps space. However, it is curious that scientists have not detected any particle that conveys the force of gravity as they have with all the other forces—for example, the photon transmits the electromagnetic force and gluons convey the strong nuclear force. These knowledge gaps and questions make physicists more convinced that there is a lot more beyond the Standard Model.

As we found earlier, nature tends to favor symmetry. If one particle is emitted to the left in one radioactive decay, another should be emitted to the right. If a particle is accelerated by the electromagnetic force, its antiparticle should move in the direction that is the mirror image of the particle when influenced by the same force. In fact, the most glaring asymmetry in the universe is the direction of time. In most physics theories, events should unfold equally plausibly whether time is going forward or backward. (For example, it's easy to think of a ball falling to the ground, or being thrown into the air.) In reality, the universe breaks the rules of symmetry—some things are not symmetric in time (for instance, a cracked egg will not reassemble itself), which is why many movies look so funny when they are run backwards. Nevertheless, all in all, nature favors symmetry.

In the 1980s, physicists started to wonder about the most fundamental parts of nature—the particles of the Standard Model—and asked if they really did explain everything. Looking at some of the questions listed earlier, physicists began to suspect that there might be more to the way the universe works than they had yet seen. The more they thought about it, the more they realized that there might be even more particles out there—not just a few more, but possibly many more. In fact, in what became known as **supersymmetry** (abbreviated SUSY), every known particle would have a counterpart; these supersymmetric counterparts could, in theory, hold the answer to many of the big questions in physics. The only problem was that these proposed new particles were huge, with masses ranging from 100 to 1,000 times as heavy as a proton. By comparison, a lead atom—with 82 protons, 124 neutrons, and 82 electrons—has a mass of about 206 times that of a proton. A single supersymmetric particle could have as much as 5 times the mass of an entire lead atom; this seemed implausible to many physicists.

Another obstacle to supersymmetry is that it is hard to test in the laboratory. At the time it was proposed, there was not a single particle accelerator in the world that could reach the energies needed to produce supersymmetric particles. Without a way to test the model, there was no way to show whether or not it could be true, and most scientists distrust a model that can't be tested. Thus, until a large enough particle accelerator could be built, supersymmetry remained an interesting idea that might solve many of these problems in physics—but it still needed testing. Luckily, with the recent construction of Europe's

Can an Accelerator Cause the End of the World?

Virtually every time a new accelerator comes online, a certain segment of the population wonders if it will cause the end of the world. People have worried about the formation of "strangelets" that might convert everything into matter consisting of strange quarks. They have worried that the high energy density might cause the vacuum to destabilize, that "baby" universes might be created, and even that mini-black holes might be formed that could swallow Earth. And, every time, these fears have come to naught.

These fears are not necessarily silly—particle accelerators do create extreme conditions that have not occurred naturally since shortly after the birth of the universe. A beam of protons circulating through the LHC has about as much energy as a locomotive moving at over 100 miles (160.9 km) per hour, and all of the energy of these protons is crammed into an incredibly small area in a vanishingly short period of time. It is only reasonable to wonder if such a high concentration of energy might cause some problems. For this reason, it is not uncommon for physicists to do some calculations first, to try to satisfy themselves that they are not endangering the world. So far, there have been no concerns.

One thing, too, that physicists bear in mind is that ultra high-energy collisions take place here on Earth, even without particle accelerators. A few times each year, cosmic rays collide with atoms in our atmosphere with energies that put even the LHC to shame. A single atom, propelled to almost ludicrously high speeds by cosmic sources that are still beyond our understanding, can have as much energy as a hard-thrown baseball. When this atom smashes into the atoms of our atmosphere, the energy released is far higher than can be generated in any particle accelerator that exists, or that is likely to exist, on Earth. If these collisions have not yet caused Earth (or the universe) to end, then our accelerators are not likely to do so, either.

Large Hadron Collider (LHC), a test for supersymmetry may be on its way. The LHC is designed to reach the incredibly high energies needed to produce many of the supersymmetric particles predicted by SUSY. If any of these particles are seen, it will be a clear confirmation of physics beyond the Standard Model. No wonder physicists all over the world are holding their breath, just waiting for the LHC to reach the energies that are needed to produce supersymmetric particles.

If the LHC does start churning out supersymmetric particles, we are in for a slew of new names to learn, many even stranger than those we have learned already. Every previously known particle—from neutrinos to quarks, gluons, and electrons—would have a new supersymmetric counterpart. Neutralinos, squarks, gluinos, selectrons, and more, might enter the jargon to find a place alongside the particles with which we are already familiar.

STRING THEORY AND EXTRA DIMENSIONS?

In addition to some of the problems mentioned earlier in this chapter, particle physics suffered from what, at first glance, seems more like a math problem—dividing by zero. Physicists have usually assumed that electrons or quarks are "point particles," meaning particles that are vanishingly tiny dots. There is certainly no reason to think otherwise and, for the most part, this assumption works well. The problem begins when trying to find out the strength of various forces as one draws closer and closer to a particle. The electromagnetic force, for example, changes with the inverse square of the distance to an object (including an electron). Therefore, to find the strength of the electromagnetic force a centimeter from a wire, for example, take the force 100 times farther away from the wire, and multiply it by 100^2, or 100 x 100, to find that, at 1 cm (or about one-third of an inch), an electric field is 10,000 times as strong as one at 1 meter (3.2 feet). However, what happens when the new distance is 0? Dividing any number by 0 gives an answer of infinity, and physicists are not happy with the idea of a force that is infinitely strong. Either there was a problem with the inverse square law, or particles had to have some actual size.

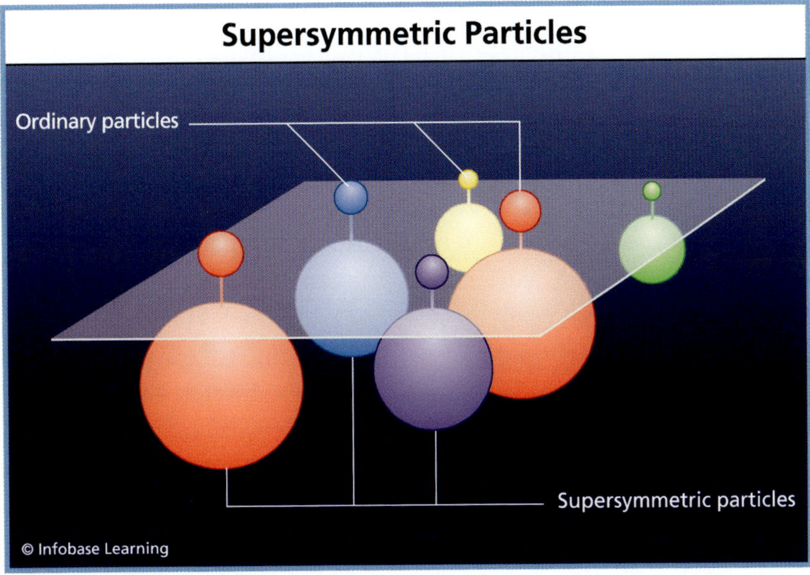

Figure 9.1   Supersymmetry requires every type of particle to have an associated supersymmetric particle.

Sometime in the 1960s, physicists began to think that their assumption of the existence of point-like particles might be too simple. What if, they wondered, the most fundamental particles (electrons and quarks, for example) were more like vibrating strings? This would certainly get them past the problem of having a size of 0, which would (hopefully) take care of the infinities that they didn't like. At first, however, the theory was not very successful, and string theory fell out of favor when physicists developed quantum chromodynamics—the theory of the strong force that holds together quarks in the nucleus. String theory came back later in the 1980s, thanks to better mathematical tools and a better understanding of how the theory could work.

After more work performed by hundreds of physicists, string theory really began to take off. At the same time, though, physicists were realizing that, while the theory seemed to solve many problems in physics, it was also growing quite complex. If physicists were going to accept a theory that could help to explain gravity and that had none of the inconvenient infinities, they also had to accept a theory that called for the universe to have more—many more—than the three dimensions of space that we are used to. In fact, to accept that all matter may be made of tiny strings, physicists eventually had to accept a universe that had a total of 11 dimensions (1 dimension of time and 10 of space). The only way that they could do this was to assume that most of the dimensions were "compactified," meaning that they existed, but were simply too small for us to notice. And that is a concept that really needs to be explained. Here's the thinking: Picture a single thread on a sewing machine (like any of the tens of thousands of threads that go into making a shirt). If a friend holds up a thread, say on the other side of the classroom, it will look like a simple line. At that distance, the thread can barely be seen at all, and it looks just like a line, having only one dimension (length). Up close, of course, the strings are three-dimensional. The naked eye can see the string has a second dimension (width), and a magnifying glass can reveal that a single thread is, indeed, three-dimensional. It is only from a distance that it looks one-dimensional; from a distance, the other two dimensions are too small to see—this is what is meant by "compactified."

Extending this to the three dimensions of normal space, scientists reason there can be extra dimensions beyond the three that we can sense; as with the thread, these extra dimensions are so small that we simply cannot detect them. This means that the familiar three dimensions are more like constructing a brick from tiny dots: We can see a three-dimensional brick, but what we cannot see is that every single dot is also, in its own right, a three-dimensional object. So, the three dimensions of this brick of dots would actually have nine dimensions because each of the three dimensions that we see is also fully three-dimensional. This is important because the strings predicted by string theory are so small that they can vibrate in all of these dimensions.

String theory cannot yet be tested in the laboratory. No present-day tools or instruments are capable of detecting these very small extra dimensions; no accelerators are capable of producing the energy to test string theory. However, if accelerators detect supersymmetric particles, it will provide important support for string theory, as string theory requires the existence of these particles (though alternatives to string theory can require them, too). So, although string theory seems to answer on paper most of all of the biggest questions in physics, unless it can be confirmed by experiment, scientists will not truly know if it is an accurate model of exactly what makes up what we call matter.

THE LHC AND THE NEXT ERA OF PARTICLE PHYSICS

Our eyes can see things that are about as wide as a hair; anything smaller is just too small to see clearly. To see anything smaller, we need help. Magnifying glasses can reveal things about the size of large cells, and ordinary microscopes can show the inside of cells. To see a virus calls for building an electron microscope, and to see molecules and atoms requires an atomic force microscope. Scientists build these instruments to extend the range of the human senses; the harder it is to see something, the bigger and more expensive are the required tools. "Seeing" subatomic particles is so difficult that it requires the biggest and most expensive tools ever made: particle accelerators.

The LHC is the biggest and most powerful particle accelerator in the world. (Before that, the Tevatron at the Fermi National Accelerator Laboratory held that distinction.) With particle accelerators, scientists tend to want the biggest and most powerful machines they can find because they need the high energies the machines provide to probe inside the atom and to create the new particles they're searching for. The next question is "Why?" For the answer to that question, it is necessary to go back a few chapters.

First, remember Einstein's discovery that matter can be turned into energy, and that energy forms matter? This is very real and has been well documented. It is also important to remember that many of the particles that physicists are looking for have very high masses, up to 1,000 times the mass of a proton. To create something so massive out of pure energy, physicists must have a powerful accelerator: a machine that will generate the very high energies needed to create these particles. Without these high energies, physicists simply cannot create the particles that will help to confirm (or not) their

Figure 9.2 This photo shows the scale of the LHC. The area under which the tunnel for CERN's LHC can be found is shown near Geneva.

hypotheses. To be clear, this is one reason to have the largest and most powerful accelerators possible: to make the massive particles that are thought to be present.

Another reason for creating these powerful machines deals with the forces within the atom itself. The force that holds quarks together to form neutrons and protons is very strong, and it takes a tremendous amount of energy to overcome this force—in other words, to "break" a proton into quarks. To "see" quarks, scientists have to be able to "hit" the proton or neutron hard (just as it takes a great deal of energy to hit a rock hard enough to break it open). The most fundamental particles are, again, the hardest to detect, requiring the most powerful tools.

As of 2011, the LHC is the largest and most powerful set of "eyes" humanity has yet developed. It has to be; its goal is to create particles that are so massive that they haven't existed freely since very shortly after the Big Bang. If these particles are found, their discovery will not only confirm some fundamental parts of the Standard Model, but may even cause scientists to move beyond the Standard Model by discovering particles that could point the way toward supersymmetry, hidden dimensions, and more. In fact, as delighted as physicists will be if the LHC confirms existing theories, some have said that this development may also be somewhat disappointing. Many physicists would dearly love to see results that are completely unexpected—something that would take physicists into new and uncharted territory.

In the past, explorers dedicated their lives to sailing beyond what was known, to explore uncharted terrain. In today's world, most of Earth has been explored, but scientists get the same thrill from exploring uncharted intellectual territory. In physics, any terrain that lies beyond the Standard Model is certainly unexplored territory, and physicists are as eager to explore this territory as Captain Cook was to explore the vast unknown of the Pacific Ocean.

At the very least, the LHC should be able to create and identify the Higgs particle (see the sidebar). If the Higgs particle is found, physicists will finally begin to understand the origins of mass. They may learn why it is that matter weighs anything, and why (for example) electrons weigh so much less than protons. Finding the Higgs particle will be a great accomplishment, and it will help to complete the Standard Model and, not to mention, likely earn a Nobel Prize for those involved. Still, there is more to the LHC than just chasing prizes.

Right now, the "landscape" of particle physics is the Standard Model, and the Higgs particle—the last undetected particle in the Standard Model—lies just barely beyond the horizon. Physicists are fairly certain that it is there, and just a little more work should bring

Mr. Higgs's Particle

One of the most interesting questions in physics is "Why does anything weigh anything rather than nothing?" On the face of it, this seems a silly question—everything that is made of matter has mass, and the question as to why it does seems almost nonsensical. To a physicist, however, this is nothing to take for granted. Consider that photons and gluons have no mass at all, some neutrinos have very little mass, and some flavors of quarks are incredibly massive. It seems natural to ask "Why?"

One possibility, first raised by Scottish physicist Peter Higgs, is that there might be some field that permeates the universe that interacts with particles passing through it; and this field is presumably carried by a particle that is now called the Higgs particle. Higgs thought that particles traveling through this field might not all interact with it in the same way; some particles might be resisted more than others. One way to think about this would be in terms of objects moving through air. For example, when you wave a fairly small stick through the air, there is little air resistance at all. It is easy to do. However, it is not always easy to wave a kite through the air; the large, relatively flat surface of the kite causes a lot of air resistance and makes it harder to wave around than a stick. This is why kites can fly and sticks don't: Kites provide more resistance to the air.

In just the same manner, Higgs proposed that different particles feel more resistance to the Higgs field than others. If Higgs is right, the reason that photons have no mass is that they just don't feel the Higgs field. At the same time, neutrinos and electrons presumably have a very weak interaction with the Higgs field, and some quarks interact quite strongly indeed. This, according to Higgs, explains why anything weighs anything at all.

it into view, but the real excitement is what else might come into view along with the Higgs particle. To extend this analogy somewhat, the Higgs particle may be a lone peak standing in the middle of a flat plain of the Standard Model, or the Higgs particle may be the first foothill of an entirely new range of mountains that will also come into view at the higher energies the LHC provides. If the latter is the case, scientists may find that the LHC opens up an entirely new world of particle physics, possibly giving us even more understanding of how our universe, and all of the matter and energy in it, is constructed.

Glossary

antimatter Particles that have the same mass and size as their matter counterparts, but whose other properties, such as electric charge, are opposite

atom The basic building block of matter, made of a positively charged core (the nucleus) surrounded by negatively charged electrons

atomic mass unit (amu) A unit for measuring the mass of an atomic or subatomic particle; the lightest atom, the hydrogen atom, has a mass of about 1 amu.

atomic number The number of protons in an atomic nucleus

binding energy The energy that is released when two atoms, or two nuclei, bind together

black hole An object with such a strong gravitational pull that no matter can escape it

chemical energy The energy that comes from chemical reactions, specifically the rearrangement of electrons in atoms and molecules after chemical reactions

conduction The transfer of energy between objects in direct contact with one another

conservation of energy The principle that energy in the universe is neither created nor destroyed

convection The transfer of energy that occurs when a hot object moves to a colder object

cosmologist Scientist who studies the origin, evolution, and ultimate fate of the universe

dark energy A form of energy, perhaps coming from space itself, that is pushing the universe outward

dark matter Matter that does not radiate any form of light and cannot be seen

electrical energy Energy that comes from the flow of electrons or other electrically charged particles

electrons Negatively charged particles that surround the nucleus in an atom and which participate in chemical reactions

energy The capacity of an object to do useful work

gas A group of atoms or molecules that has no definite shape and tends to spread out in all directions when released from a container

general theory of relativity The modern theory of gravity, developed by Albert Einstein, which describes how the universe behaves at large scales where gravity dominates

geothermal energy The heat energy that comes from below the surface of Earth

gluon Particle that carries the strong force and holds together quarks as well as neutrons, protons, and other groups of quark-containing objects

heat energy A general form of energy associated with the random motions of particles at elevated temperatures

Higgs particle A particle hypothesized to exist everywhere in space and give other particles the particular masses that they have

Hubble Constant A quantity that provides information on the age of the universe and how quickly it is expanding

kinetic energy The energy of motion

liquid An object that tends to flow but does not spread out like a gas when released from a container

mass A quantity that defines the amount of matter in an object; the more mass an object has, the harder it is to push and the heavier it is in a gravitational field.

matter Anything that occupies space and contains mass

molecule A group of atoms held together by chemical bonds

neutrino An invisible, hard-to-detect particle with very low mass that carries away energy in nuclear reactions

neutron   Particles in the nucleus that have zero electric charge

nuclear energy   The energy stored in the nucleus of an atom

nucleus   The positively charged core of an atom

pair production   The conversion of pure energy into a pair of particles, such as an electron and positron

phase transition   A transformation from one state of matter to another, such as the melting of a solid into a liquid

photon   A particle of light; carries the electromagnetic force

plasma   A gas of electrically charged particles

positron   The antimatter version of an electron

potential energy   The amount of energy stored in an object

power   The rate at which energy is produced by an object or system

proton   Positively charged particles that exist in the nucleus

quantum mechanics   The theory that describes the world at the scale of atoms

quark   Building block of protons, neutrons, and other objects held together by the strong force

radiation   The transfer of energy or particles through space, such as sunlight reaching Earth

solar energy   The energy that comes from the Sun or any other source of light

solid   An object with a definite size that tends to change its shape when subjected to a force

special theory of relativity   Theory, developed by Einstein, that explains how matter behaves when it travels near the speed of light

Standard Model   The highly successful, but seemingly incomplete, current description of the particles and forces in nature

superconductivity   Complete disappearance of electrical resistance in a substance, especially at very low temperatures

supersymmetry   A theory that predicts that all known particles and antiparticles have yet-to-be-detected heavier counterparts, known as superpartners, such as the squark and neutralino

wind energy   The energy that comes from wind as it turns a turbine to create electricity

Bibliography

Calder, Nigel. *Einstein's Universe*. New York: Gramercy, 1988.

Davies, Paul. *The New Physics*. Cambridge, U.K.: Cambridge University Press, 1992.

Greene, Brian. *The Elegant Universe: Superstrings, Hidden Dimensions, and the Quest for the Ultimate Theory*. New York: W.W. Norton and Company, 1999.

Halliday, David, Robert Resnick, and Jearl Walker. *Fundamentals of Physics*. New York: Wiley, 2004.

Hawking, Stephen. *The Illustrated Brief History of Time, Updated and Expanded Edition*. New York: Bantam, 1996.

Sagan, Carl. *Cosmos*. New York: Random House, 2002.

Schwarz, Cindy and Sheldon Glashow. *A Tour of the Subatomic Zoo: A Guide to Particle Physics: Second Edition*. New York: American Institute of Physics, 1996.

Singh, Simon. *Big Bang: The Origin of the Universe*. London: Fourth Estate, 2005.

Further Resources

Einstein, Albert and Nigel Calder. *Relativity: The Special and the General Theory.* New York: Penguin Classics, 2006.

Greene, Brian. *Icarus at the End of Time.* New York: Knopf, 2008.

Hakim, Joy. *The Story of Science: Einstein Adds a New Dimension.* Washington, D.C.: Smithsonian Books, 2007.

Hawking, Stephen. *The Universe in a Nutshell.* New York: Bantam, 2001.

Seife, Charles. *Alpha and Omega: The Search for the Beginning and End of the Universe.* New York: Viking, 2003.

Teresi, Dick, and Leon Lederman. *The God Particle: If the Universe Is the Answer, What Is the Question?* Boston: Mariner Books, 2006.

Trefil, James. *The Nature of Science: An A–Z Guide to the Laws and Principles Governing Our Universe.* New York: Houghton Mifflin, 2003.

Wiker, Benjamin, and Jeanne Bendick. *The Mystery of the Periodic Table.* Bathgate, N. Dak.: Bethlehem Books, 2003.

Web Sites

CERN: European Organization for Nuclear Research
http://public.web.cern.ch/public/
> *This site offers information about the Large Hadron Collider, a major international facility that aims to detect new particles and even extra dimensions.*

Fermilab Virtual Tour
http://www.fnal.gov/pub/about/tour/index.html
> *Here is an online tour of the Fermi National Accelerator Laboratory in Batavia, Illinois.*

How Things Work
http://howthingswork.virginia.edu/
> *This site provides answers to questions about physics, science, and how things in the world around us work.*

Particle Adventure

http://www.particleadventure.org/

Take an interactive tour of quarks, neutrinos, antimatter, extra dimensions, dark matter, accelerators, and particle detectors.

Physics Central

http://physicscentral.org/

This site from the American Physical Society shows how physics is a part of the everyday world.

Symmetry Magazine

www.symmetrymagazine.org

This online magazine discusses particle physics and its connections to other aspects of life and science, from collaborations to policy and culture.

Index

A

accelerators, 59, 103, 106, 107–111. *See also* Large Hadron Collider
adaptive optics, 91
Alhazen, 38, 39
Al-Khazini, 38
Alpha Centauri, 77
annihilation of radiation, 7
anti-electrons. *See* Positrons
antihydrogen, 36
antimatter
    Big Bang and, 14
    energy and, 51
    overview of, 34–35
    symmetry and, 82–83
antiparticles, 66–67
antiprotons, 34–35
Aristotle, 38
asymmetry, 14, 102
atomic bombs, 7, 49, 53
atomic mass units (amu), defined, 15
atomic number, 60
atoms
    chemical energy and, 46
    overview of, 11–13
    parts of, 59–63
    size and, 18–19

B

baby universes, 103
background radiation, cosmic microwave, 74, 75
baryons, 71
batteries, 28, 45
beauty quarks, 70, 73
beta radiation, 63–64
Bhagavad Gita, 60
Big Bang, 14, 74
Big Crunch, 91, 96
"big rip" scenario, 98–99
binding energy curve, 51, 52–53
black holes, 75, 84–86
Book of Optics (Ibn al-Haytham), 39
Bose-Einstein condensate, 56
bosons, 65, 66
bottom quarks, 70, 73
brick analogy, 11–13

C

carbon atoms, size of, 18
Casimir effect, 58
Cepheid variables, 92, 94
CERN (European Organization for Nuclear Research), 15–16

Chandra X-ray images, 76, 85
charge, 60–61, 72
charm quarks, 70–71, 73
chemical energy, 24, 25, 28, 40, 46
chemical potential energy, 43
classical physics, defined, 40
clay analogy, 11–13
closed systems, 40
closed universe, 96–97
colors, star composition and, 92
combustion, 40, 46, 47
compactification, 106–107
conduction, defined, 79, 80
conservation of energy, 24, 40–42, 58, 63
convection, defined, 79–81
cosmic microwave background radiation, 74, 75
cosmic radiation, 68–70
cosmologists, defined, 74, 96
counterweights, 28, 29, 45
crystals, liquid, 22
Cygnus X-1, 86

D

dark energy, 9, 10, 91–98
dark matter, 9–10, 88–91
Democritus, 59
Digitized Sky Survey, 85
dimensions, extra, 106–107
Doppler shift, 92, 94
down quarks, 70, 73

E

E=mc², 35, 48–49, 56, 82
Earth, gravitational field of, 53
Einstein, Albert, 7, 9, 35, 55, 69. *See also* E=MC²
electrical energy, 24, 25, 44–46
electrical generators and motors, 32
electromagnetic energy, 78–79, 101
electromagnetic fields, 46
electron neutrinos, 57, 64
electron volts, 49
electrons
  atomic structure and, 60–62
  mass of, 57
  pair production and, 56
  photons, positrons and, 7–8
  as point particles, 104
elevators, counterweights and, 28, 29, 45
energy
  definitions of, 24–28, 38–40
  power and, 36

energy fields, overview of, 30–34
European Organization for Nuclear Research (CERN), 15–16
expansion, of universe, 92–98
extra dimensions, 106–107

F

Fermilab, 73
fields, 16, 31, 110
fission, defined, 52
flat universe, 96–97, 99
flavors, quarks and, 71
food, 43
friction, heat energy and, 79
fuel, antimatter as, 36
fusion, 28, 30, 51–52, 74–75

G

Galileo Galilei, 31, 88
gas, plasma as, 22–23
gasoline, stored energy and, 30
Gell-Mann, Murray, 73
general theory of relativity, 101
generators, electrical, 32
Glashow, Sheldon, 73
gluinos, 67, 104
gluons, 66, 72–73
graphite, 18
gravitational field, mass of, 53
gravitational potential energy, 38, 45, 77–78
gravity
  bending of light by, 101

black holes and, 84–86
energy and, 26–27
general theory of relativity and, 101
Great Attractor, 76
Greece, 40, 59

H

heat energy, 24, 46–47, 79
helium, superfluid, 55
Higgs, Peter, 16, 17, 110
Higgs bosons, 66
Higgs particles, 16–17, 109–111
Hiroshima, 7, 49, 53
Hoover Dam, 26–27, 28–30
Hubble, Edwin, 92, 96
Hubble Constant, 91, 92–93, 94
Hubble Space Telescope, 76, 91
hydroelectric power plants, 26–27
hydrogen atoms, 15, 19, 27–28, 30

I

Ibn al-Haytham, 38, 39
ice, melting of, 20–21
interchangeability of matter and energy, 7–8, 10
Io, 46
ionizing radiation, defined, 37
Isgur, Nathan, 72

J

Joule, James, 38
joules, defined, 36
Jupiter, 46

K

Kepler, Johannes, 88
kinetic energy, 30, 38, 40–44, 79
kites, 110

L

Laplace, Pierre-Simon, 84
Large Hadron Collider (LHC)
  energy of beam of protons in, 103
  Higgs particles and, 15–16, 109
  purpose of, 59
  superpartners and, 67, 104
leptons, 65, 66
Leucippus, 59
LHC. *See* Large Hadron Collider
light
  bending of by gravity, 101
  color of, star composition and, 92
  as pure energy, 7
  speed of, 48, 49, 76
light bulbs, 36–37
light matter, 75
liquid crystals, overview of, 22

M

magma, 81
magnetars, 32–33
magnetic fields, 31, 32–33
mass, 14–15, 43–44
mechanical energy, 28
mesons, 71
Michell, John, 84
microwaves, 78–79
molecules, overview of, 11–13

Moon, gravity of, 77
mortar and brick analogy, 11–13
motion, kinetic energy and, 30, 38, 40–44, 79
motors, electrical, 32
muon neutrinos, 64
muons, 57, 66, 69

N

neutralinos, 104
neutrinos, 57, 63–68, 89–91
neutron stars, 75
neutrons
  atomic structure and, 60–63
  defined, 15
  mass of, 57
  nuclear energy and, 46
  particle accelerators and, 108–109
  quarks and, 70–73
Newton, Isaac, 77, 88
Nobel Prizes, 56, 73, 82–83, 109
Northern Lights, 23, 68
nuclear energy, overview of, 46
nuclear fission, defined, 52
nuclear force, strong, 61, 72–73, 101
nuclear fusion, 28, 30, 51–52, 74–75
nuclear power, defined, 25–26
nucleons, binding energy curve and, 51
nucleus, defined, 15

O

open universe, 96–97, 99

orbitals, atomic structure and, 60–62
orbiting objects, laws governing, 88

P

pair production, 53, 56, 57, 58, 82
particle accelerators, 59, 103, 106, 107–111. *See also* Large Hadron Collider
PET (positron emission tomography) scanners, 50–51
petroleum, 26
phase transitions, 21–22
photinos, 67
photons
  electromagnetic force and, 66
  electrons, positrons and, 7–8
  energy from, 79
  pair production and, 53, 56
planets, pull of, 77
plasmas, overview of, 22–23
point particles, 104
positrons
  beta radiation and, 63–64
  electrons, photons and, 7–8
  overview of, 34–35
  pair production and, 56
potential energy
  conservation of energy and, 40–42
  gravity and, 27
  overview of, 42–43
  as storage of mechanical energy, 28

power, energy and, 36
protons
  atomic structure
    and, 60–61
  defined, 15
  mass of, 57
  nuclear energy and,
    46
  particle accelerators
    and, 108–109
  quarks and, 70–73

Q

quanta, 63
quantum mechanics,
  101
quantum physics,
  defined, 40
quark confinement, 73
quarks, 65, 70–73, 75,
  104, 108–109

R

radiation, 7, 34–37,
  79, 80
radioactive decay, 66
refining, petroleum
  and, 26
relativity, theories of,
  69, 101
reservoirs, 28–30

S

selectrons, 104
singularity, 84
size, overview of,
  17–20
solar flares, 32
solar storms, 46
solar wind, 68
solid state, overview
  of, 20–21
sources of energy,
  25–26
special theory of
  relativity, 69

Spitzer Space
  Telescope, 76
springs, potential
  energy and, 28, 42
squarks, 104
SS-433, 86
Standard Model of
  particle physics, 17,
  65–67, 100, 102,
  109–111
stars
  black holes and,
    74–75, 84–86
  conduction,
    convection,
    radiation and, 81
  electrical energy
    and, 46
  expansion of, 92
  laws governing
    motion of, 88–90
  magnetic fields and,
    31–33
states of matter,
  overview of, 20–23
static electricity, 40
stellar-mass black
  holes, 86
stored energy,
  overview of, 28–30
strange quarks, 70, 73,
  103
strangelets, 103
string theory, 104–107
strong nuclear force,
  61, 72–73, 101
subatomic particles,
  mass of, 57
Sun
  electrical energy
    and, 46
  magnetic fields of,
    31, 32
  as plasma, 23
  pull of, 77
  solar wind and, 68
super-atoms, 56
superconductivity, 54
superfluidity, 54–55

super-massive black
  holes, 86
supernovae, 68, 94,
  97–98
superpartners, 66–67
supersymmetry
  (SUSY), 102–104
symmetry, 14, 82–83,
  102

T

tau neutrinos, 64
tau particles, 66
telescopes, 76, 91
temperature, 54–55
tetraquarks, 71
Thales, 40
time, 36, 69
top quarks, 70–71, 73
transfer of heat and
  energy, overview of,
  78–81
truth quarks, 70–71,
  73
turbines, energy and,
  26–27, 30
Type Ia supernovae,
  94

U

universe
  composition of, 9
  effects of energy in,
    82–83, 86
  effects of matter on,
    75–78
  expansion of, 92–98
  fate of, 98–99
  reason for presence
    of matter in, 82–83
up quarks, 57, 70, 73
uranium, 26, 30, 52

V

Van Allen radiation
  belts, 68
velocity, 43, 88–89

virtual particles, 58
visible light, 36, 37

W

W particles, 57, 66
water, 13, 16, 26–27
watts, defined, 36

waves, Bose-Einstein condensate and, 56
weak nuclear force, 101
weight, energy and, 9
WIMPs (Weakly Interacting Massive Particles), 91

Y

Young, Thomas, 38

Z

Z particles, 57, 66

About the Authors

P. Andrew Karam is a scientist, writer, and educator who has devoted himself since 1981 to radiation safety. He received his Ph.D. in Environmental Sciences from Ohio State University. He has written more than 100 technical articles and editorials in scientific and technical journals and newsletters. He has also authored over 200 encyclopedia articles and several books, including *Rig Ship for Ultra Quiet*, which describes his first encounters with radiation science as a Navy technician on a nuclear submarine. He lives in New York City.

Ben P. Stein has been a professional science writer since 1992. He earned his bachelor's degree with honors at the State University of New York at Binghamton. He then attended journalism school at New York University, where he embarked upon a career in science writing. He worked at the American Institute of Physics for 16 years. His writing has appeared in *Encyclopedia Britannica*, *Popular Science*, *New Scientist*, *Salon*, and many other publications. He lives in Columbia, Maryland.